The Think Tank

The Think Tank

100 adaptable discussion starters
to get teens talking

MARTIN SAUNDERS

MONARCH
BOOKS
Oxford, UK, & Grand Rapids, Michigan, USA

First published in the UK in 2010 by Monarch Books
(a publishing imprint of Lion Hudson plc)
Wilkinson House, Jordan Hill Road, Oxford OX2 8DR, England
Tel: +44 (0)1865 302750 Fax: +44 (0)1865 302757
Email: monarch@lionhudson.com
www.lionhudson.com

ISBN 978 1 85424 964 7

Distributed by:
UK: Marston Book Services, PO Box 269, Abingdon, Oxon, OX14 4YN
USA: Kregel Publications, PO Box 2607, Grand Rapids, Michigan 49501

British Library Cataloguing Data
A catalogue record for this book is available from the British Library.

Printed and bound in Malta by Gutenberg Press.

Contents

For Joel and Naomi

Introduction

Story

Story is everywhere. We create it, consume it, and take part in it every day. Story is important – it helps us to make sense of our lives, the world around us, and each other. We understand life as a story, and we use story to describe that life to one another. Whether it's in our consumption of media, our conversations with friends or even our own inner monologues, story is an irremovable element at the heart of humanity.

God understands this. More than that, he is the "Great Storyteller". He is constantly creating it in millions upon millions of ways, every day. Every human life carries the divine spark of creativity not only in the creation of another unique individual, but in the story that individual goes on to map out over the course of their life. So this is life on Earth: billions of stories, all constantly crossing over into one another; connecting; combining; clashing; giving meaning to each other. Imagine viewing that from God's perspective – truly the most complicated plot line in literary history!

God the storyteller chose to communicate with us through story. We sometimes take for granted that the Bible is not only a record of God's engagement with humanity; it's also a peerless work of literature. God could have chosen simply to write us a list of regulations for following Him, but instead he chose to breathe life into a great library of stories – filled with heroes, villains, sex, violence, intrigue, sacrifice, and most crucially of all, redemption.

One of the key purposes of *The Think Tank* is to give young people an opportunity to meet that incredible Bible narrative – perhaps for the first time. This volume of discussion starters contains 100 creative suggestions for helping to open up accessible entry points to scripture – not because the Bible isn't interesting or powerful enough to speak for itself, but because recent generations have not, for the most part, been instilled with an appreciation of just how relevant and vital it is.

Yet, as central as the Bible is to the Christian life, it is only part of the story. The Old and New Testaments give us huge insights into thousands of years of the history of God's people, but they rarely stretch into the infinite distances either side of that period. God is and has always been (a tricky concept for me, I'll confess); his story did not begin with the creation of man. Similarly, the story of God's people didn't end with the lives of the apostles. Incredibly, the faith survived against all odds, and now takes in an estimated two billion followers worldwide. Thanks to Jesus, we have an eternal story to look forward to, as co-heirs of the everlasting Kingdom of God.

Youth workers have a role to play in helping young people to understand the extraordinary idea that they have a role to play in God's unfolding story. This epic journey that takes in every Bible character and story from Genesis to Revelation – which weaves through the lives of every saint, martyr and hero of the faith and inevitably ends up in glory – somehow, somewhere we have a role to play in it. Essentially, though it might sound a little glib, working out our part in God's story is the meaning of life itself.

Stories

Young people display a huge appetite for stories. Whether consuming book after book in the latest vampire or wizard saga, downloading movies (legally and otherwise) or immersing themselves in photo-realistic video games, teenage interest in stories has arguably never been greater. They learn about the world, about imagination and creativity, about right and wrong, from stories – and, of course, this can sometimes be very dangerous.

It's not just fiction that captures the teenage imagination, however. With the advent of the Internet, people young and old were given greater access than ever before to a proliferation of stories, in a number and breadth that would previously have seemed impossible for one person to reach. Again, this had wonderful applications and terrible ones – users could reach into the lives and the stories of people all over the world; yet, they also had almost totally unregulated access to uncensored sex, violence and depravity, at levels from which most people would previously have been shielded.

The Internet as we know it today, however, is a very different beast to that of a decade ago. The most fundamental change came with the arrival and establishment of Web 2.0 – the point at which the Internet ceased to simply be a gigantic uncensored library of information, and became defined by its participants. "We are the Internet" is the phrase coined by a professor at the University of Kansas, and he was correct – with the rise first of blogging, user-generated content websites such as YouTube, and latterly social networking sites such as Facebook and Twitter, the Internet has been given a human brain.

What social networks in particular have given rise to is something that digital experts call "the grand meta-narrative". What that means is that there is a huge, complex, billion-participant story being created and recreated every day in the middle of the Internet. People take the interesting (and sometimes not so interesting) elements of their everyday lives and post, blog, tweet or upload them to the Internet where they become public property, creating an opportunity for others to respond. Blog comments, YouTube reviews and Twitter trends are all examples of how this meta-narrative – the giant super-story – begins to take shape. This is fuelled partly by traditional computer use, but increasingly through portable devices such as mobile phones. Today's young people are a hyper-connected generation because they are *always* on – or seconds from accessing – the web.

There is a problem with this, however, and it's a strange extension of the phenomena that the first wave of the Internet brought. When chat rooms, instant messenger services and forums first appeared, experts were concerned that young people were retreating into a "digital shell", where they would choose online friends over physical ones, and hide behind a partly fictionalized "avatar", pretending to be someone else. For the most part, that didn't really happen; some marginalized young people chose to do this, but the majority maintained physical friendships as well as virtual ones.

What's happened now, however, is that physical relationships are being continued at a lower priority than online ones. Young people see their mobile device as an extension of themselves – an inseparable body part – and check it regularly for updates on their social network profiles. Even if they are at dinner with a friend, enjoying coffee with a parent or youth worker, or even taking part in a church service or youth work session, they will dip out of that conversation intermittently to take a look at their phone. What they are implicitly communicating, at that point, is that this physical social situation is of a lower priority than "the grand meta-narrative" taking place online. On one level, they are always plugged in to the stories that are unfolding online as people post updates, videos, comments, and more. One of the reasons why this is of concern is that online communication is usually a reductionist version of a real relationship. Twitter asks us to sum up our part in the story at any moment in just 140 characters; people become bored by blog posts that are more than a few sentences.

I believe youth workers need to actively teach and emphasize the importance of physical community and face-to-face relationship. Discussion is a great way of modelling this, and I would urge you to use this book as a way of creating a deeper sense of community among the groups of young people with whom you use it.

100 stories

This book contains 100 stories designed to provoke discussion, and each is accompanied by a number of questions designed to aid you in facilitating that. The 100 are split into four equal sections, which I will outline below. In the first volume of adaptable discussion starters (*The Ideas Factory*), I decided to make the last 25 slightly different to the first 75, by creating a 25-step journey through the "grand story" of the Bible. Readers very kindly commented that this added extra value to the resource, so I have tried to do something similar again. This time, though, the final 25 discussion starters are based not around a read story, but around a video clip. All of the films are available on DVD – most of them for under £5 – so hopefully this will again make for some extra value to you the youth worker.

These discussion starters are intended to help you to get young people talking, to engage their sense of story, and to point them towards the bigger story that's not just confined to a book, but going on all around them.

Each discussion starter is presented in the same format: a discussion trigger, and three banks (two for the film clips) of questions.

The **discussion trigger** is a short story or, in the case of film discussions, an introduction which you can either read to your young people, give to them to read, or both. There is huge variety in these; they are intended as a "tin-opener" and little more, and don't go into great detail. You may wish to add some words of your own to flesh them out, but I have deliberately made them brief, as experience tells me that while young people like to hear a story, they don't particularly want a three-point sermon. In the case of the film clips, I would recommend you read the summary provided, play the clip, and then move on to the questions.

Each discussion trigger opens up at least one theme, which is then unpacked in the questions below it.

The **Opening up** questions are designed to spark the discussion into life. They are generally lower in impact, although you may still see the conversation catch fire! These questions are not always of a spiritual nature, and are more likely to refer to the story in the discussion trigger.

The **Digging deeper** questions (not applicable to section D) tie more directly to the main theme, and are not aimed specifically at Christians. No assumptions are made about faith; these questions are designed as a tool for you to use in guiding and facilitating conversations. You may wish to provide your own answers to these, pointing more directly at the Christian perspective, but they do not explicitly refer to spiritual themes.

The **Taking it to the Word** bank of questions are a Bible study, mainly aimed at Christian groups, or young people who are interested in exploring Christianity. They are not intended for use with young people who have made no such suggestion. It is important to note that not all of these question banks leave the group with a nice, neat conclusion – it's up to the group facilitator to draw things to a close in a way that he or she sees fit.

The book is divided into four sections, each containing 25 discussion starters. These are:

- Would you believe it? – Often unbelievable stories; all absolutely true.

- Inspiring individuals – Stories of celebrities, public figures, and other people of note, making a positive difference in the media spotlight.

- What would you do? – Ethics are explored through true and semi-fictional stories, many of which are based on real events. Names have been changed to protect the innocent and the guilty!

- Talking movies – A bonus element: 25 movie clips that "pack a punch" with young people, and all the background and questions you'll need to facilitate discussion around them.

Adapting and other preparation

This book is intended as a resource, but I strongly recommend that you do not view it simply as a "get-out-of-jail-free" card, to be pulled out at the last minute and used as is. To get the most out of the discussion guides, and to really make them work for your group, I suggest you take some time ahead of your meeting to adapt the words for your context. This might mean slightly changing the wording, or adding or removing questions.

If you are working with non-churched young people, for instance, you may wish to delete the "Taking it to the Word" questions completely, or reduce their number. If you have a longer session, you may wish to add your own questions in the "Digging deeper" section. Think hard about your audience, and which areas of the discussion you feel will help or interest them most. I also advise that you treat subjects such as family, self-image, and sexuality with extra caution, and try to anticipate any questions which might create an uncomfortable or upsetting situation for some of your young people.

That's it – you're ready to go. Take this resource, pull out the best bits and leave the parts that don't work behind. You know what your young people will respond to far better than I possibly could, so don't be afraid to edit, adapt, and rework. I hope you find it helpful as you seek to build community, stimulate thought and get young people talking.

SECTION A:
Would you believe it?

Introduction

The best true stories are the ones you simply could not make up. Those tales that sound so tall that when they are relayed to friends, they are invariably met with a half-believing cry of "no way!"

My own life seems to be littered with these sorts of experiences. I have accidentally insulted the wives of important business people, been caught apparently filming a man standing at a urinal, and even found myself accidentally DJ-ing in a Chicago nightclub without any knowledge of the equipment. Every time I have retold one of those stories, my audience has responded with a mixture of amazement and disbelief. But for exactly those reasons, these are the kinds of memorable anecdotes that stick in the minds of everyone who hears them.

This first section contains 25 discussion starters around just this sort of memorable story. From the tale of the four-year-old expelled from school, to the story of Nina Petre, the Romanian pet psychic, each contains that vital element of "unlikeliness" that will catch a teenager's imagination and draw them in to conversation.

Here's a promise: every one of these stories is absolutely true and has been confirmed by at least two separate news sources. Occasionally, I have changed the names to protect the unwitting, but the tales themselves are all genuine. It's important that you know that before you start – because inevitably young people will challenge you on it!

These discussion starters are particularly suitable to use in school assemblies and "God slots", because they involve real people. The "Digging deeper" questions take a theme or issue into more detail, so this bank of questions could be especially useful in a school lesson or after-school club context. As ever, for best results, you should take time before your meeting to adapt the resource for the young people with whom you will be using it.

Don't try to use all the questions (unless things are going really badly!), and if it doesn't feel appropriate, don't force the scriptural element in. There's plenty of value to be had around the thematic issues suggested, even if you don't get on to the Biblical discussion. Above all, have fun, and see these 25 resources as a tool for relationship – not for forcing a Christian viewpoint on an issue.

Oh, and as for the urinal story – I was actually checking the football results while waiting to use the bathroom in an Indian restaurant. Turned out I was holding my camera phone at an incriminating angle, and the man standing in front of the lens did not accept that explanation. He went straight back into the restaurant and announced in a loud voice that there was a pervert making videos in the toilet. I emerged to learn this a few moments later.

You couldn't make it up.

A1

THEME: **False prophets**

BIBLE: **1 Kings 18**

I see dead pitbulls

The death of a pet can sometimes be as difficult for an owner to bear as the loss of a friend or relative. Animal lovers can build up deep attachments to their pets, sometimes over a period of ten or twenty years. Parents even use those morbid final trips to the vet as a dry run to get the children ready for when Grandma departs the earth.

But for all those who have lost a favourite guinea pig and never got the chance to say goodbye, help is possibly at hand. Romanian psychic, Nina Petre, offers to contact the spirit of your recently snuffed-it pet, for a fee of course. Cynics might suggest that she is taking advantage of grieving pet owners in their greatest moment of vulnerability, but Nina claims that she really does have a hotline to doggy and moggy heaven. Communicating with clients through a website, she promises to send your message on to the spirit world – and to get a response (presumably translated from the original bark, squawk, or meow).

Petre's website quotes one formerly healthy dog, named Mexico, as telling her owner, "I want to let you know that I am very happy here. I just came from the dogs' judgment where I was told my good behaviour in life means I have a good chance to be sent back. But I couldn't have done this without your support, wisdom, and love for which I will always be grateful to you. I also have one wish. Please give all my stuff – collar, leash, and little coat – to a new dog which I know you will love as much as you did me."

Man's best friend to the very end, and beyond.

OPENING UP

- How do you think Nina Petre came up with her message from "Mexico" (the dog)?

- What do you think would have been the owner's response?

- Does it matter if Nina is a fake or not?

DIGGING DEEPER

- Psychic prediction is big business. Why do you think people use psychics? Could there be truth in their claims?

- If not, how do you think psychics sometimes achieve such accurate results?

- What do you think is the difference between a psychic and a prophet?

TAKING IT TO THE WORD

Read 1 Kings 18:22–40

- How do you feel about this story? Does the ending feel harsh? Why or why not?

- Do you believe God can "send fire" in your life, in the way that he did here?

- Pray together for the discernment to know real prophets from false ones, and for the faith to step out from the crowd like Elijah did.

A2

THEME: **Smoking**

BIBLE: **1 Corinthians 6**

The four-year-old chain smoker

Whatever your views on smoking, you probably agree that there's a minimum age below which people shouldn't try cigarettes. For some, that will be the legal age (16 in the UK), and for others it will be sometime earlier in the teenage years. Few people would sympathize with the family of Dong Dong, a Chinese boy who was already an established smoker at the age of four.

Dong shocked doctors during a routine examination, when they discovered what they called "a long history of smoking", possibly stretching back to when he was just two. The boy lives with his grandparents in China's Anhui province, where the old couple run a grocery store. The shop sells cigarettes, and the owners say they have been unable to prevent Dong from stealing cigarettes from it. They say he started smoking because he was trying to mimic adults.

"When he needs cigarettes, he just takes them from the house or steals a pack from the store. We just can't seem to stop him," said Dong's grandmother.

Doctor Zhang Gong, from Anhui Provincial Children's Hospital, said that Dong's habit was incredibly dangerous. "From the way the boy smokes, and his posture, he looks to have had a long history of smoking even though he is so young," he said.

Local reports suggest that Dong also drinks alcohol, and that he learned to walk and talk later than the rest of the children in his village.

OPENING UP

- Do you picture Dong as a young "urchin", or as a victim? Why?

- Do you sympathize with his grandparents (Dong's parents are migrant workers overseas)?

- What impact do you think Dong's habit will have on other children in the village?

DIGGING DEEPER

- What are your views on smoking? Should it be banned completely? Are smokers already penalized and persecuted far too much?

- Why do people smoke? What makes a person start smoking?

- If someone you know was trying to give up smoking, how would you help them? Which approaches would be helpful, and which wouldn't?

TAKING IT TO THE WORD

Read 1 Corinthians 6:19–20

- What does it mean that our bodies are "temples of the Holy Spirit"?

- How do you feel when you read "you are not your own"? Do you find that difficult at all?

- How should these verses affect what we put into our bodies? What other implications does this have, besides the one about smoking?

A3

THEME: **Watering down the story**

BIBLE: **Hebrews 5–6**

Beyond a yolk

They have been a part of childhood since the Middle Ages, but it seems that for some people, nursery rhymes are no longer suitable for children. That's certainly the impression you would get if you watched children's TV channel CBeebies, who have been changing the endings to traditional rhymes in order to give them a happier ending.

Take "Humpty Dumpty" for instance; in the well-loved original version, Humpty smashes to pieces after falling off a wall, and even the combined skills of the king's army are unable to piece him back together. However, in a new version rewritten for CBeebies pre-school viewers, the final line is: "All the king's horses and all the king's men made Humpty Dumpty happy again."

Labour MP Tom Harris, who watched the broadcast with his two children, criticized the change. "Kids should be exposed to real life a bit, not cosseted away," he said. "Let them see colourful and violent cartoons, and let them be children!" He also claimed that he's seen the ending of "Little Miss Muffet" changed so that she and the spider ended up as friends.

Meanwhile, education campaigner Nick Seaton told *The Sun* newspaper: "Nursery rhymes are a gentle way to ease children into the real world. Children are being told everything is rosy and aren't being raised to confront problems."

OPENING UP

- Do you think nursery rhymes should be changed so they don't upset small children? Why or why not?

- Do you agree with Nick Seaton that children are not being raised to confront problems? Why would that be a problem, if so?

- When do you think it's best to protect people from bad news? When might it be very important that we don't?

- When is it tempting to water down bits of the Christian message?

DIGGING DEEPER

- What do you understand by the term "political correctness"?

- When is it a positive idea? When can it be less positive?

- Do you think the Christian message can be offensive to people? How?

- Should Christians be quieter about some of their beliefs in public? Which ones? How do we decide?

TAKING IT TO THE WORD

Read Hebrews 5:12 – 6:12

- These verses seem quite harsh. How do you feel about some of the things Paul says here? What strikes or concerns you?

- How do we reach maturity as Christians?

- What does it mean to train yourself to distinguish good and evil?

- Why is verse 10 reassuring?

21/10/12
cw

A4

THEME:　　**Making judgments**

BIBLE:　　**John 7**

What's in a name?

English teachers have traditionally warned their pupils not to judge a book by its cover. But are they and their colleagues in the staffroom really practising what they preach? Apparently not, if a recent survey is to be believed.

According to a poll by the Bounty parenting club, teachers believe they are able to predict which children in a class will be badly behaved, just by looking at a list of their names. More than a third said they expected pupils with certain names to be more disruptive, and almost half admitted they made assumptions about a child when they first looked down the register.

Teachers were particularly likely to judge boys in this way. So if you are called Callum, Connor, Jack or Daniel, be warned. You are on the watch-list before you even step into a classroom and throw your first paper plane. Girls didn't get away scot-free however; Chelsea, Chardonnay and Aleisha also made the top ten.

The survey also asked teachers to suggest the names of typically bright pupils, and concluded that Alexander, Adam, Elizabeth and Charlotte were among those most likely to be destined for Oxbridge. And while they may not be the brainiest, Charlie, Emma and Hannah were likely to be the most popular members of any class.

The respondents were defended by Bounty spokeswoman Faye Mingo – judge that name however you wish – who claimed: "It's only natural for teachers to make judgments based on the behaviour and performance of former pupils with the same name, but I'm sure that they are happy to be proved wrong."

OPENING UP

- How does this story make you feel? Are teachers justified in thinking this way?

- Compile your own list of naughty or popular names. How would you feel to be on one of those lists?

- What could the effects be of branding someone "naughty", "clever" or "popular" simply based on their name?

DIGGING DEEPER

- What do you think of your own name? What does it mean to you?

- Do you know what it actually means? Does that meaning fit you?

- If you had to change your name, what would you change it to and why?

TAKING IT TO THE WORD

Read John 7:24

- How do we avoid judging a book by its cover? What practical steps can we take to achieve that?

- What is a "right judgment"? What criteria should we use?

- Who have you judged on appearance alone? Pray that God will give you specific opportunities to give people second chances, see beyond appearances, and make "right judgments".

A5

THEME: **Gender roles**

BIBLE: **Ephesians 5/Galatians 3**

The manageress

Imagine the scene. It's 2052, and England have just won the World Cup for the sixth time. The players take turns to hold the trophy aloft, until finally their manager – the brilliant tactical genius who has masterminded their success in the tournament – appears. The president of FIFA, the grey-haired David Beckham, extends his wrinkled hand towards that manager. Warmly he exclaims: "Well done, Mrs Powell."

What about a woman managing the England football team? Could such a thing ever happen? Right now, such an idea seems ridiculous, but as equality of opportunity continues to be achieved in many other areas of employment, perhaps it's not such a crazy idea.

Especially since, in 2009, one woman made history by becoming the first member of her sex to lead out a semi-professional British football team as manager. Donna Powell was ordinarily a turnstile operator at lowly Fisher Athletic, who play their matches in the Blue Square South division. However, after raising £500 for the club, the 27-year-old, who was already the manager of an under-11s boys' team, was given the opportunity to manage the first XI for one match.

Struggling Fisher had already lost ten games in a row before Donna took over, and although they lost her game in charge 2–1, the performance of the team was a credible one, with the all-male playing staff following her coaching instructions to the letter. With her team losing 2–0 at half-time, Donna made tactical changes which almost saved the game.

"I wasn't happy with the way my team played in the first half," she said afterwards. "It was too comfortable for them, but during the interval I switched the formation to 4–4–2. Two banks of four to bolster the defence and I put on an extra target man to try and put the defence under pressure. The response from the players was very pleasing and Rausy scored a terrific goal near the end. I thought we were a little unlucky not to nick a draw but for the rub of the green."

With a firm grasp of footballing cliché already under her belt, Donna now only needs to take her coaching badges, which she is currently studying for. "Donna wasn't just anyone," explained the Fisher Athletic chairman. "She loves this club; she's put in the hard work and proved to the board she has the right credentials. Donna's now seen what's involved and if she continues on this path, gains further experience and takes those coaching badges, she can do a job in football."

OPENING UP

- What is your honest response to the idea of a top-level woman football manager? Could it work? Why or why not?

- What might be some of the immediate problems a woman would face in coaching a professional men's team?

- How do you think the players would have reacted to Donna's one-match appointment as Fisher manager?

DIGGING DEEPER

- Are there some jobs that can only be done by men or women? Why?

- Do you think sometimes the campaign for gender equality goes too far? Why or why not?

- How would you feel if you were told you couldn't vote because of your gender? What would you do?

TAKING IT TO THE WORD

Read Ephesians 5:18–33

- These verses seem to suggest that women should submit to men in the context of marriage. What then does it mean to "love your wife as Christ loved the church"? What did Christ do for the church that husbands should replicate?

Read Galatians 3:25–29

- These verses suggest that there is "no male or female" – that we are "all one in Christ Jesus". Is this a contradiction of the Ephesians verses, or are the two statements somehow working in harmony?

- Pray together that God will give you his perspective on gender, and that you will seek to be people who are for justice and against prejudice and discrimination.

A6

THEME: **Connectivity**

BIBLE: **Acts 2**

Marital status update

Over the past few years, social networking websites have become incredibly popular. People frequently stop what they are doing, whether they are on the go or sitting at a computer, to update their Facebook, Twitter, and other accounts. Usually, that's not inappropriate – particularly since a survey revealed that the most popular place to make an update was sitting on the toilet!

Sometimes, however, the physical friends around you can feel quite rejected when you interrupt your actual conversation with them in order to update your virtual friends. So spare a thought for the bride of an unnamed groom, who stopped his wedding ceremony in order to update his Facebook profile.

The man pulled out his phone the moment after the minister had pronounced the couple man and wife, in order to change his marital status on the site from "in a relationship" to "married". Then he handed his new wife her phone so that she could do the same. He even found time to send an update to Twitter, tweeting, "Standing at the altar with Tracy Page where just a second ago, she became my wife! Gotta go, time to kiss my bride!"

The minister and congregation apparently found the whole thing hilarious. Hopefully, the marriage will be successful, and the process will not be repeated (in reverse) in a divorce court – but if it were to sadly come to that, you wouldn't put it past them...

OPENING UP

- What's your initial feeling about this story? Is what happened funny; inappropriate; worrying?

- Why do you think the groom chose to do this?

- Why do people like to update their social networking profiles? What's the attraction?

DIGGING DEEPER

- How important is it for you to feel connected?

- How and when do you update your social networking profiles? At home? In public? Why do you tend to do it at these times?

- Do you ever break off from conversations in order to do this? Do people do this to you? How does it make you feel?

TAKING IT TO THE WORD

Read Acts 2:42–47

- This is a description of the early church. How similar is the church of today?

- What do you think the outside world would make of a church like this? Would they think it was insane, or be queueing up to join? Why?

- These Christians were totally connected to each other in a profound way. How many people are you really connected to?

- How can you make sure that your online connections don't become more important than your real friendships?

A7

THEME: **Ecology**

BIBLE: **Genesis 2**

The magic roundabout

With a growing population, people are finding more and more ingenious solutions to shortages in housing. Few, however, can rival the endeavours of one homeless woman.

Not only did Sharon Simpson create a luxury tent home for herself in the middle of a busy city-centre roundabout; she did it all without anyone knowing she was there! Using immense resourcefulness, and after sorting through piles of the stuff that other people had thrown away, she created an oasis for herself that included a TV, DVD player, and even a solar-powered shower.

Mrs Simpson had been on the brink of eviction from her house, after rows with her partner had led to social services becoming involved with her family. Fearing that hostel accommodation would see her surrounded by drug addicts, she quit the property, left her children in the care of her mother-in-law, and set out to build her makeshift new home, taking only a one-person tent with her.

She discovered the well-shaded area in the middle of Derby's Pentagon roundabout island, and pitched her tent. Rooting through skips, she found items including car batteries, sun-loungers, and tent-extensions. A friend helped her to recharge the batteries, and connected up a discarded TV, DVD player and digital box.

Mrs Simpson eventually left when the leaves fell from the trees around her, meaning she was suddenly in full view of thousands of motorists a day. She moved in with her sister, which of course, begs the question of why she didn't do that in the first place. "You can find all sorts in skips," she said afterwards. "One man's junk is another man's treasure."

OPENING UP

- Ignoring some of the moral questions about her family life, what do you make of this story, and Mrs Simpson?

- What does Mrs Simpson's example possibly have to teach us?

- Why do you think she chose the roundabout over simply going to her sister's house?

DIGGING DEEPER

- How much do you think about what you throw away? Why?

- What's your attitude when things break or lose their interest for you? Do you tend to throw too much away, or reuse and recycle everything?

- Have you ever thrown anything away that would have been perfectly useful to someone else?

- Why do you think people throw away working TVs, DVD players and more?

TAKING IT TO THE WORD

Read Genesis 2:15 – in this verse the words "take care" come from the Hebrew shamar, meaning "to exercise great care over".

- How well do you "exercise great care" in the way you interact with the planet?

- Why would God care about the condition of the earth if he could just fix it if he wanted?

- How might thinking more about what we throw away help us to respond to this verse, and God's command to Adam as figurehead for all humankind?

A8

THEME: **Bearing the name**

BIBLE: **2 Corinthians 5**

Mr Monster Munch

We all have our guilty pleasures – rubbish films we secretly love to watch when no one is around, or comfort food that most other people would find unremarkable. But the plumber formerly known as Chris Hunt wasn't embarrassed by his obsession with children's snack food Monster Munch. In fact, he was so proud, he officially changed his name to reflect his passion.

Mr Monster Munch, as he's now known, is so obsessed with the snacks that he eats them for breakfast, lunch and dinner. He always starts the day with a bag of pickled onion Monster Munch – which must delight anyone he goes on to meet in the morning – then has a roast beef Monster Munch sandwich for lunch, and a packet of Flamin' Hot flavour for dinner.

Mr Munch, 26, is so in love with the corn-based food that he's also created a range of recipes to involve it in rice and pasta dishes. However, he's quick to address any accusations that he's unhealthy: "I run 35 miles a week, and train in the gym regularly," he told reporters. He also claimed to eat a "balanced diet", suggesting he doesn't *only* eat Monster Munch.

Monster changed his name by deed poll after being

dared to do so by friends. "I don't think they thought I would go through with it," he said, "but now I demand to be called either Monster or Mr Munch."

OPENING UP

- Why do you think Mr Munch is so obsessed with his favourite food?

- Do you think that – considering the depth of his love – he was justified in changing his name?

- What problems might Mr Munch now encounter as a result of his decision? Do you think he will change his name back to Chris Hunt?

DIGGING DEEPER

- What are some of your guilty pleasures, in terms of food, music, TV and more?

- What is the thing (or person!) you are most obsessed with? How deep does your obsession run?

- How far would you go to demonstrate your obsession? Would you go as far as Mr Munch?

TAKING IT TO THE WORD

Read 2 Corinthians 5:16–21

- As Christians we bear the name of Jesus Christ. How should that affect how we treat others? How might their view of that name change through how they see us behave?

- Would it be easier to be a Christian if no one else knew apart from you? Why or why not?

- What does it mean to be "Christ's ambassadors"? How can you grow into that role more fully?

A9

THEME: **Sacrifice**

BIBLE: **John 15**

My life for my friend

When you are poor, you are often also left feeling very powerless. Chinese student Dan Dan must have felt that way when her best friend, Zhang Yuemei, was diagnosed with a life-threatening illness. The treatment would cost around £15,000 – and with both girls coming from poor farming families, the idea of raising that money seemed simply impossible.

Dan Dan had already proved that she was a resourceful young woman – having achieved a place at university despite her lowly upbringing. So even though the potential medical bills were sky-high, she refused to consider the possibility of letting her friend suffer and die.

Zhang had been diagnosed with encephalomyelitis, a disease of the brain and spinal cord. Without the expensive treatment, she would deteriorate into a vegetative state, and eventually die.

Faced with the prospect of seeing this happen to her best friend, Dan Dan took the most extreme course of action – offering her hand in marriage to any man who agreed to meet the cost of Zhang's treatment.

In an online advert she wrote: "Donate [£15,000]

to help 22-year-old girl suffering from severe brain inflammation, I would repay with my body, marry the person... I am tender, obedient, understanding and know how to do house chores. Good appearance, although I am not an especially pretty girl, but I look cute, with good temperament!"

OPENING UP

- What do you think of Dan Dan's gesture? Is what she's doing noble, incredible, or going too far?

- What might you do in her position – if your friend was dying and no one seemed able to help?

- Do you think there could be an ulterior motive to her advert?

DIGGING DEEPER

- How much would you sacrifice for your best friend? Would you go as far as Dan Dan?

- What is it about friendship that means people are sometimes prepared to suffer greatly for the sake of their friends?

- What does it mean to be a great friend to others?

TAKING IT TO THE WORD

Read John 15:9–17

- Verse 13 talks about a greatest kind of love – why is that both so noble and so difficult to live up to?

- Why does Jesus make such a big deal about love here?

- How do you feel to read that Jesus calls you his "friend"?

- How has Jesus "laid down his life for his friends"?

- How should we respond?

A10

THEME: **Freedom**

BIBLE: **Galatians 5**

Awake

What's your worst nightmare? Drowning? Being attacked by insects or wild animals? Whatever it is, it's unlikely to match the horror suffered by Belgian road-crash victim Rom Houben, who was stuck in a coma for twenty-three years – and conscious all along.

Doctors had no idea that Rom, who suffered paralysis in a 1983 motorcycle accident, could hear everything that was going on around him for more than two decades. They incorrectly believed he was in a persistent vegetative state, and thought his brain functions were what they termed "extinct". In fact, they had misdiagnosed his condition, partly because at the time of his accident, technology did not exist to correctly identify what was actually wrong with him.

At last, in 2006, new hi-tech brain scans revealed the true nature of the damage suffered by Rom, and showed that his brain was functioning almost completely normally. Soon, through the use of specially adapted computer equipment, he was able to communicate with the outside world, including his family.

"I dreamed myself away," Rom said later. "All that time I just literally dreamed of a better life. Frustration is too small a word to describe what I felt. I shall never forget the day when they discovered what was truly wrong with me. It was like my second birth."

Rom was "saved" by neurologist Dr Steven Laureys. "Medical advances caught up with him," he explained. Chillingly though, Dr Laureys wrote in a medical paper that he thought there might be many other cases of these "false comas", in hospitals all around the world.

OPENING UP

- What is your immediate reaction to this story?

- How do you imagine Rom felt? How did he stay sane?

- Do you think you could draw any possible positives from being in such a condition?

- How do you think Rom now understands the idea of freedom?

DIGGING DEEPER

- What is your worst nightmare? Does it compare to Rom's ordeal?

- List some of the things you fear. What are some of the common themes among them?

- How do you avoid living a fearful life? How can you overcome things you fear?

TAKING IT TO THE WORD

Read Galatians 5:1, 13–15

- What is the kind of freedom that Paul is describing here? How does it differ from the freedom that Rom experienced? How is it similar?

- Can the image of Rom, trapped in the "false coma", help us to understand the idea of freedom in Christ?

- What do these verses tell us to do with our freedom? What will happen if we abuse it?

A11

THEME: **Creativity**

BIBLE: **Exodus 35–36**

Stair master

How do we define creativity? Usually, when we talk about creative people, we are describing artists, poets, musicians, and film-makers. But creativity is more than just a skill – it's a state of mind, as one ingenious Chinese man proved.

Budding inventor Li Rongbiao, 67, sold his apartment in order to fund his big idea – the creation of a stair-climbing wheelchair.

Li came up with the idea after his wife Wang Huifang, two years his junior, broke her leg. "It used to take us a good half an hour to walk downstairs from our fifth-floor apartment after her injury," he told the *West China City Daily*.

So, despite no prior mechanical knowledge, Li set about learning the necessary skills, and sold the couple's apartment for £44,000 to raise money for the invention.

Incredibly, Li successfully built a prototype of his invention, which requires a small amount of physical intervention to work. Already, however, he is hard at work on a revised version which he hopes will work without any assistance. He claims that his invention already climbs 3,000 steps – or 50 floors – on a single charge.

Li was asked by reporters how he had managed to build the invention without any engineering experience. "I bought a lot of books," he replied.

OPENING UP

- Why do you think Li was inspired to become an inventor in his late 60s?

- What do you think his wife would have made of her husband's decision?

- Do you think it was responsible of Li to sell their apartment? Why?

DIGGING DEEPER

- What do you think about when you hear the word "creativity"?

- In what ways do you think you are creative?

- Do you think creativity is something that everyone has? Are we born with it, or can we learn or acquire it somehow?

TAKING IT TO THE WORD

Read Exodus 35:30 – 36:2

- How are creative gifts born according to this passage?

- Where does Bezalel's creativity come from? What can that teach us about our own creativity?

- Do all skills and abilities come from God, or just those given to Christians? Explain your answer.

A12

THEME: **Sin**

BIBLE: **Romans 6**

Lost in translation

A good advertising slogan can cost hundreds of thousands of pounds. Advertising, marketing and branding experts charge heavily for their "expert" services, to help companies to come up with killer taglines like "Just Do It" and "I'm Lovin' It". In the case of both those phrases, that slogan doesn't just sell shoes or burgers in one country, but in countless territories around the world.

Coming up with a slogan that works internationally is even harder, and sometimes costs even more. So spare a thought for the tourist board of the Eastern European country of Latvia, who wasted a huge chunk of their marketing budget to a mistake in translation.

It's not hard to guess what they meant, but there was no way the campaign could go ahead when tourist bosses realized that the slogan had been mistranslated into: "Easy to go, hard to live". Unfortunately, they only noticed after the posters and other materials had already been printed.

The posters, which would have appeared in the UK and other English-speaking countries, were meant to help shake off the capital Riga's current reputation as a global HQ for wild bachelor and stag parties. The slogan was to appear next to images showcasing the city's many cultural highlights.

Instead, thanks to one simple mistake, the posters appeared to suggest that a visit to Latvia presented a great risk to freedom.

OPENING UP

- What are some of the best advertising slogans you can think of? Why do they work?

- What are some of the worst? What effect do they have on your view of that product or service?

- What are some mistakes you have made recently? Today?

- Can you think of other examples where one small mistake ruins something much bigger?

DIGGING DEEPER

- What might have been the consequences of going ahead with the mistranslated posters? Was it better to pull them completely?

- When have you made a mistake that has had negative consequences? How did you feel about them? What would you do differently in hindsight?

- What should happen to people who make small mistakes which cause big problems? Should they be punished according to the size of the mistake... or the size of the resulting problem?

TAKING IT TO THE WORD

Read Romans 6:20–23

- What does "the wages of sin is death" mean?

- How much sin can you commit before receiving punishment? What if you are mainly a good person but only sin a little bit?

- Do you think God punishes according to the size of our mistakes, or the size of the resulting problem? What is that problem? (Psalm 5:4–6 may help.)

- Why is verse 22 especially reassuring?

A13

THEME: **Marriage**

BIBLE: **Matthew 19**

Free to collect: Nagging wife

"Nagging Wife. No Tax, No MOT. Very high maintenance – some rust."

This was the actual wording of a small ad which appeared in British magazine *Trade-It,* a title more usually associated with the sale of used cars and second-hand household items. The advert was the work of Gary Bates, 38, a self-employed builder whose wife Donna had told him off one time too many for leaving the toilet seat up.

"She was nagging me for doing something small, while she was watching rubbish on TV," Bates later explained. "So I just thought I'd put an ad in to get rid of her." Of course, it was all a joke – but that didn't stop dozens of men ringing up to enquire about her availability.

"I didn't think anyone would ring up but I had at least ten people calling about her," he told reporters. "There was no one I knew – just people asking, is she still available?"

Bates placed his wife's advert in the "Free to Collect" section of the magazine, alongside some of his fishing tackle.

"She gave me a bit of an ear-bashing at first," he confessed, "but she's seen the funny side of it now." The Bates' have been married for a year.

OPENING UP

- Do you think Mr Bates' advert was a harmless joke and nothing more? Why or why not?

- Why do you think so many men rang Mr Bates in response? Were they just jokers too?

- When does a practical joke go too far? Where are the lines?

DIGGING DEEPER

- What words and phrases come more readily to mind when you think about marriage? More things like "love", "cherish" and "honour", or "nagging", "unhappy", and "divorce"?

- What has informed your view of marriage?

- Do you intend to marry? What would you like that marriage to be like? How would it be different to other marriages?

TAKING IT TO THE WORD

Read Matthew 19:3–6

- Jesus talks about married couples here – these familiar words are part of the Christian marriage ceremony. Why do you think he refers back to Eden?

- What does it mean to become one flesh – and how might that impact our view of relationships before marriage?

- Do many marriages in your experience reflect this idea of being "united"; "not two but one"? Why or why not?

- How do these verses affect your own aspirations for marriage?

A14

THEME: **Perseverance/Dreams**

BIBLE: **James 1**

950th time lucky

South Korean grandma Cha Sa-soon has the sort of never-say-die attitude that made Bill Gates a billionaire and James Bond a global icon. She doesn't build computers or shoot Russian terrorists, but she has demonstrated remarkable character in her own simple way.

Mrs Cha sells vegetables and other goods in the town of Jeonju, near Seoul, but it has been her long-held dream to take the business on the road. She decided to buy a van in order to increase the scope of her business, but there was a problem... she couldn't drive. Like many others, the South Korean driving test comprises both a written and a practical element.

On the practical side, Mrs Cha was fine, but the written test struck fear into her heart. As it turned out, she was right to be afraid – she failed the test over and over again. And then over, and over, and over again. She spent more than 5 million won (the Korean currency, approximately £2,600) on application fees for the test.

Talking to the media after what was – incredibly – her 775th failure, Mrs Wan appeared undeterred. She told reporters that she would simply keep taking the

50-question test until she reached the pass mark of 60 per cent. "I believe you can achieve your goal if you persistently pursue it," she said.

And, of course, she was right. Neatly, her success came on attempt number 950. Workers at the Jeonju test centre, where she had become well known, were overjoyed. "Her challenging spirit is amazing," said one.

Now she just needs to pass the practical test...

OPENING UP

- Do you think Mrs Cha is inspirational... or crazy? Why?

- What do you think of her quote: "you can achieve your goal if you persistently pursue it"? Do you think she's right?

- What might have been some of the reasons behind Mrs Cha's persistence?

DIGGING DEEPER

- No laughing allowed. What's your biggest dream? Do you want to be a movie star? See the world? Change it?

- How realistic do you believe that dream is? Could you get there? Why or why not?

- What do you think Mrs Cha's approach to that dream would be? How would she practically attempt to make it come true?

TAKING IT TO THE WORD

Read James 1:2–8

- James is talking about persevering through trouble and suffering, but how can his words also be applied to more positive situations?

- How can you possibly find "joy" in failure and setbacks?

- How does perseverance create maturity – and what does that mean?

- What can you take from this passage that can help you to achieve your own ambitions?

A15

THEME: **Answered prayer**

BIBLE: **Matthew 7**

Ring and a prayer

Ohio pastor James Ng had planned his marriage proposal meticulously. He had saved for months for the $3,000 engagement ring; booked an incredible flight on a hot air balloon during which he would pop the question; and convinced his unsuspecting girlfriend to take flight with him.

But when the camera bag in which he had hidden the ring accidentally fell overboard, the plan suffered a serious setback. James was horrified as he watched the bag (which also contained his camera) plummet 500ft into woods below. Seeing the severity of his reaction, girlfriend Sonya Bostic realized what was going on – so James dropped onto one knee and proposed anyway, using a handy piece of ring-shaped plastic.

Sonya said yes, and upon landing the couple drove to the local Wal-Mart to pick up a temporary $5 ring. Even though the bag had fallen into dense woodland, however, James refused to accept that the ring he had spent so long saving for was lost forever. For the next week, he and a friend searched through the undergrowth, armed with machetes to cut back the thick brambles.

After seven days of praying and searching the

three-square-mile area where the bag might have fallen, James did indeed find the bag. The camera had been taken, but the ring was still inside. Overcome with emotion and excitement, James took the ring straight to Sonya – appropriately, it was a perfect fit.

OPENING UP

- What do you think the odds are that James Ng would a) find the bag, and b) find that someone had taken the camera but left the ring behind?

- Do you think James' prayers had anything to do with his seemingly lucky discovery?

- Why do you think James didn't give up his search, even after six fruitless days?

DIGGING DEEPER

- What is prayer? Do you do it/have you ever done it?

- Do you believe prayer works at all? If so, in what way? If not, why not?

- Do you think prayer has other benefits even if maybe it isn't really a connection to God?

TAKING IT TO THE WORD

Read Matthew 7:7–12

- Does this sound like prayer as you have experienced and understood it? Why or why not?

- How does "everyone who asks receive"? Is that true?

- How can we sometimes play down the power of prayer?

- Pray together boldly, asking in faith for the things that you would really like to see in the lives of your friends, your community and in your own life, and realizing that you are talking to your heavenly father – creator of the universe.

Dave Ritter
7/10/12

A16

THEME: **Righteous anger**

BIBLE: **Ephesians 4**

Wind assistance

A footballer playing for lowly Manchester football team Chorlton Villa may have the dubious distinction of being the only player ever to be given a yellow card for breaking wind.

An opposition striker was running up to take a penalty kick when the player suffered a noisy gas release, but when the penalty was then saved, the referee ordered it to be retaken. He cautioned the offending player, citing rules against "ungentlemanly conduct", and insisted that the penalty taker had been put off by the sheer volume of the fart. This time, the striker for International Manchester FC scored, and in doing so changed the course of the game.

Chorlton went on to lose 6–4, and afterwards their manager Ian Treadwell was mortified by the referee's decision. "The other player had the penalty saved because it was a bad penalty," he said: "It was nothing to do with any noise."

The referee's decision to book a player on the basis of a "wind release" saw the game descend somewhat into farce, as three players became so angry that they ended up with red cards. "While I don't condone the actions of the players," Mr Treadwell continued, "it is an emotive game and some of the players were sent off for entering into a conversation with the referee."

"We're not a dirty team," he insisted.

OPENING UP

- Do you think the referee was right to caution the player and have the kick retaken?

- Do you sympathize with the Chorlton players who got sent off? Why or why not?

- Why do you think they allowed their team to be reduced from 11 to 8?

DIGGING DEEPER

- How often do you get angry? What are some of the things that make you cross?

- What can be some of the negative outcomes of your anger?

- Is it sometimes justifiable to get angry? In what circumstances?

- What could be some more positive outcomes of anger?

TAKING IT TO THE WORD

Read Ephesians 4:26–32

- Paul talks about a kind of anger without sin – what kind of anger is this? How is it possible to separate anger from sin?

- Why should you not go to bed angry though?

- Why is verse 29 a really helpful way of measuring what kind of anger we are feeling?

- How do verses 31 and 32 help to balance the picture? What should we look like as Christians?

LIGHT CANDLE / prayers. / tealights.

✓ av 19/11/12

A17

THEME: **Drugs**

BIBLE: **Romans 6**

Grassed-up by a toddler

Having a child can mean you sleep less, have a reduced social life, and spend most of your time talking about nappies. One of the less common side-effects of having a baby, however, is that they inadvertently bring down your criminal empire.

That's what happened to one Canadian father though, after his 11-month-old son accidentally "called the police". Randomly punching buttons on the phone his dad had given him to play with, the little boy called the emergency service number, 911. Concerned by the silent call, police sent Mounties to the home in White Rock, British Columbia.

This was especially unfortunate because "dad" was a major-league cannabis grower, with over 500 plants in his home-made "farm". When the Mounties arrived at his door, they received no answer and decided to break in. Inside, the bemused father had no idea why they had received a 911 call from his property, but the police pieced the mystery together when they again found the child playing with the phone.

By this stage, however, they had caught scent of the unusual odour emanating from the man's house.

The officers conducted a full search, during which they uncovered two locked rooms containing the marijuana plants.

The man was later jailed. Child welfare officers placed the boy with his mother, who had separated from the man.

OPENING UP

- Do you find this story funny, sad, or both? Why?

- What do you think the man felt after losing his son? How might he feel about drugs in the light of his loss?

DIGGING DEEPER

- What do you think are acceptable and unacceptable drugs? Where do you draw the line?

- Do you think too much is made of the dangers of drugs? Do you think young people get patronized and talked down to on this subject?

- What are some of the non-health related effects – good and bad – of drug use?

TAKING IT TO THE WORD

Read Romans 6:11–13

- How much care do you take of your own body? How much do you think about what you put into it?

- What does it mean to let "sin reign in your mortal body"?

- What do you think these verses say about drugs?

A18

THEME: **Wisdom**

BIBLE: **Proverbs 4**

At least I'm not hired

If you were hoping to be considered for a new job, you might well take care not to offend your potential new employers. No one had given this glaringly obvious piece of advice to young Englishman James Kettle, however, when he was busily writing off for roles in the tourist industry.

When horticulture graduate James applied for a job at the National Botanic Garden of Wales, things got off to a fairly bad start as he accidentally sent his emailed application to the Aberglasney Gardens in Carmarthenshire – a completely different Welsh attraction. Much less forgivably, James made his application using the email address "atleastimnotwelsh".

His request was met with a snappy reply from a manager at Aberglasney, who wrote: "It may be prudent to change your email address. It could have a detrimental effect on any career aspirations of working in Wales."

James, who had been in his final year as a student in Warwickshire, said afterwards that he felt "a right fool". "I set up the email at school because several Welsh kids were in my year," he sort-of explained. "I forgot it was on my application, and I didn't mean to be offensive."

Shockingly, James didn't get the job.

OPENING UP

- How do you think James felt when he realized his mistake?

- Why would he have used this email address in the first place? Did he get his just deserts or was it just harmless fun?

- In what ways do you think James will learn from this humiliating experience?

DIGGING DEEPER

- When have you made bad decisions? How might you have made better ones?

- What does it mean to be wise? Is it something you aspire to? Why or why not?

- How do you think we can become wiser?

TAKING IT TO THE WORD

Read Proverbs 4:6–7

- What does "wisdom is supreme" mean? And what does it mean to "love" wisdom?

- Verse 7 claims that getting understanding will "cost all you have". Why?

- How do we become wiser people? (James 1:5 may help.)

A19

THEME: **Money**

BIBLE: **1 Timothy 6**

Cavedog billionaires

Forty-something Hungarian brothers Zsolt and Geza Peladi were so poor, they lived in a cave. By night they would huddle together in the freezing cold, hoping that they would both make it through until morning. By day, they would sell scrap they had found in the street for pennies.

What the brothers didn't realize, as they went about their fairly miserable lives, was that they stood to inherit an amount so large that they could barely imagine it. Far away, in Germany, the brothers' maternal grandmother was sitting on an estimated £4 billion fortune.

So when the old lady died – and thanks to a German law which automatically entitles direct descendants to a share of any estate – the search began to find her family. That quest ended when homelessness support workers in Budapest found the brothers, selling their scavenged wares at a local market.

"We knew our mother came from a wealthy family but she was a difficult person and severed ties with them, and then later abandoned us and we lost touch with her and our father until she eventually died," Geza explained. "We don't know yet if she even told our grandmother about us – I understand it was only while they were carrying out genealogical research that lawyers found we existed."

Geza was also optimistic about how his newfound fortune might change the brothers' lives: "If this all works out it will certainly make up for the life we have had until now – all we really had was each other – no women would look at us living in a cave. But with money maybe we can find a partner – and finally have a normal life."

OPENING UP

- What do you imagine your life would be like if you lived in a cave in an otherwise developed country? How might people treat you?

- How do you think the brothers felt when they heard about their inheritance?

- Do you think they were 100 per cent excited – or would they have had reservations?

DIGGING DEEPER

- Do you think money will solve all the brothers' problems? Why or why not?

- Why would having money make Geza think he would find a partner? What kind of relationships might this view lead to?

- What would you do with £4 billion?!

TAKING IT TO THE WORD

Read 1 Timothy 6:6–10

- What is "godliness with contentment"? How do we achieve it?

- What do these verses suggest about money? Do you agree with the "wisdom" in these verses?

- How do you think the average person would view these verses? Would they agree or disagree?

- Can money be a good thing? When and how? Pray together, that you will be wise in the way you use your money, and never fall in love with it.

A20

THEME: **True value**

BIBLE: **Matthew 13**

The diamond dog

Dog ownership is now a phenomenon in China, creating major problems in already over-crowded cities where one-dog-per-family laws have been introduced.

That's unlikely to present a problem for one super-rich dog owner in the Chinese province of Shaanxi, however. One would imagine the woman, Mrs Wang, has quite a substantial garden in which to exercise her recently purchased pooch. Why? Because Mrs Wang paid around £350,000 for the animal.

For that astronomical outlay, Mrs Wang was rewarded with the delivery of a Tibetan mastiff with the catchy name of Yangtze River Number Two. The dog's new owner had reportedly spent years scouring China for the "perfect mastiff". When she found it in Yangtze River Number Two, she continued to up her offer to the dog's previous owners until they were simply unable to say no.

The price was a world record, dwarfing the previous most paid for a dog. That £90,000 expense was only generated when a family in Florida paid to have their much loved (and recently deceased) Labrador cloned.

Yangtze River Number Two's arrival in Shaanxi was

greeted like a state visit, as a fleet of luxury cars arrived at the airport to collect it. Mrs Wang's wealthy circle of friends sent limousines, and also arranged a huge welcoming party of banner-wielding dog lovers.

Surrounded by reporters, the dog didn't make any comment on the welcoming committee, but did complain that its flight across China was a bit "ruff".

OPENING UP

- What's your initial reaction to this story?

- Is Mrs Wang's outlay immoral with so much poverty in China? Or do you think she's entitled to spend this sum on a dog?

- Why do you think Mrs Wang was looking for the "perfect mastiff"?

- Do you think she will be pleased with her purchase, and consider it good value?

DIGGING DEEPER

- What would you spend a fortune on? A house? A car? Something else?

- Do you aspire to be rich? Why or why not?

- If you were super-rich, and had everything, how do you think you would feel?

TAKING IT TO THE WORD

Read Matthew 13:44–46

- How sensible or ridiculous do these very short stories sound to today's listener?

- What parallels are there with Mrs Wang's story?

- Why do the people in all of these stories spend such incredible amounts on something seemingly small?

- What do you think Jesus is getting at in these stories? What is "the kingdom of heaven"?

- How are we all called to "sell all we have" in pursuit of the kingdom?

A21

THEME: **Remembrance**

BIBLE: **Joshua 4**

Coach Hitler

In 1930s Germany, he was a familiar face on the touchline of football pitches across the land. Track suited and super-fit, with his trademark side parting and smart moustache always immaculately groomed, the man with the initials "AH" emblazoned on his training kit was one of the best-loved football managers in the country. Meet Adolf Hitler, one of the greatest soccer coaches Germany ever produced.

Sound right? Let's hope not. Yet, for one in twenty British schoolchildren, that's the mental picture that the name Adolf Hitler conjures up. In truth of course, Hitler is one of the most reviled figures in history, and as the architect of the Jewish Holocaust, rightly so. Yet, according to a survey, around 5 per cent of kids in Britain – the country which went to war to stop Hitler just a few decades ago – actually believed he was a German football manager.

In addition, an incredible one in six respondents to the poll – by a veterans' charity – believed Auschwitz was a theme park rather than a Nazi concentration camp, and one in twelve thought the Blitz was the post-war clean-up operation.

At least 2,000 children aged nine to eleven were

asked a series of questions in the week leading up to Remembrance Day, which 40 per cent of them had never heard of. Major Jim Panton, the Chief Executive of Erskine, who commissioned the survey, said that the results "shocked" him, and demonstrated the importance "not just of caring for veterans, but of educating society".

"Children are the future of the country," he added. "It is important we help them learn about our history."

OPENING UP

- Do you find it shocking that children don't know key facts about the World Wars? Why or why not?

- How much interest do you have in learning about history? Why does it either bore or intrigue you?

- Why is it important that the truth about things like the Holocaust is passed down between generations?

DIGGING DEEPER

- How do you react to stories of the war? Do they shock or affect you in some other way? Do they seem distant and unreal? Something else?

- How would you feel if you were asked to go to war now for your country? What would you do?

- Should we continue to remember people who died in the war, or should there come a point when we decide to stop? Explain your answer.

TAKING IT TO THE WORD

Read Joshua 4:1–9

- Why did the Israelites set up standing stones?

- Why was it important that the stories of God's miraculous acts were relayed to their children?

- What kinds of "standing stones" do we have today?

- Why is it important to remember the things that God has done in our lives? Why is it also important to remember tragedy and failure?

A22

THEME:　　**Adultery**

BIBLE:　　**Matthew 5**

Sorry, you're breaking up...

It was supposed to be a birthday treat from a wife to a husband, but in the end one phone call brought down their marriage.

When Croatian Jasna Ivanovic realized that her husband Davor was going to be away on business on his birthday, she planned what she imagined would be a brilliant surprise. She made contact with the producers of Davor's favourite radio programme, and persuaded them to call her husband live on his birthday.

Unfortunately, when the phone rang, Davor was in the shower. DJ Barbara Kolar was getting ready to hang up – assuming that the stunt had failed. Then, a woman answered the phone, and explained that Davor was in the bathroom.

When Davor came on to the phone, he tried to claim that the woman in his room was his wife. Unfortunately for him, his real wife was listening in on another line. "Who are you with?" she screamed, at once destroying the façade. Stunned, Davor shouted angrily at the DJ: "Why have you done this to me? We have kids."

OPENING UP

- Do you think Davor had any grounds to be angry with the DJ? Why or why not?

- How might you have felt listening to that broadcast?

DIGGING DEEPER

- What are your views on adultery? Can it ever be justified? Is it unrealistic to expect people to be faithful forever?

- What counts as an "affair"? Can people commit adultery without having a sexual relationship?

- Why do you think so many people commit adultery? Do you think the world views it as unacceptable, or understandable?

TAKING IT TO THE WORD

Read Matthew 5:27–30

- These are incredibly strong words. Do they sound too harsh in the context of today's world?

- Does Jesus mean we should really cut parts of our bodies off? If not, then what does he mean?

- How do you respond to Jesus' words on lust? Do they shock you? Again, does he really mean what he is saying here?

A23

THEME: **Self-image**

BIBLE: **Psalm 139**

Fat ankles Barbie

When a famous French shoe designer was asked to create three new Barbie dolls for the character's fiftieth anniversary, most people expected to be wowed by his clothing designs. But the real shock came when Christian Louboutin decided to redesign the actual doll because he thought her ankles were "too fat".

There has often been controversy around Barbie dolls, with some politicians and campaigners believing that she is too thin and sends out the wrong message to young girls, that they should look the same. Until now, however, she's never been criticized for carrying *too much* weight.

That changed when Mr Louboutin, whose shoes can cost more than £1,500, came to design footwear for his versions of the doll, and decided she had what he calls "cankles", or chubby ankles.

A spokeswoman, clearly carried away by all the glitz and glamour of the industry, told the media that the dolls are "completely wild and even come with little Louboutin boxes for the shoes. But he found her ankles were too fat." Let's all hope her feet don't snap off. The doll's feet, I mean.

OPENING UP

- What messages do you think Barbie dolls give to young girls? Are they harmless fun?

- Do you see anything wrong with Mr Louboutin's decision to thin Barbie's ankles?

- Why do you think the fashion industry seems so obsessed with skinny women? Is it their fault, or partly ours?

DIGGING DEEPER

- How happy are you with your own body? Would you change anything?

- What factors help you to develop your self-image – your own idea of how good or bad you look and come across to others?

- Do you know people with a low self-image? How does that make you feel? What would you like to say to them about that?

TAKING IT TO THE WORD

Read Psalm 139:1–16

- This passage describes how God sees us. What are some of the key verses?

- How should these words – if they are really true – affect the way we see ourselves?

- What's your favourite line in this Psalm and why?

- Pray together, that God will help you – and others who struggle with a poor self-image – to see yourselves as God sees you.

A24

THEME: **"Crime" and punishment**

BIBLE: **Ephesians 6:14**

Expelled at four

At what age do we know right from wrong? If the staff at Sacred Heart Primary School in Preston are to be believed, then four is definitely old enough. The story of now-former pupil McKenzie Dunkley – expelled in his first term as a four-year-old – suggests that if you are old enough to start school, you are also old enough to be thrown out of it.

McKenzie, one of the youngest children ever to be expelled, had only been at school for a few weeks when his behaviour was deemed unacceptable. Teachers said that he was violent, disobedient, prone to distracting other children, and always running out of the classroom. The final straw came when he allegedly "assaulted" a teacher for a second time. He was sent home from school four times, and eventually expelled from the school.

The boy's mother, Shelley (who gave permission for her son's name to be made public), insisted that her son had previously displayed no behavioural problems. She told reporters that the school had "made him out to be a thug", despite the fact that he had never displayed any problems at nursery.

She continued, "He's still only four and getting used to school. There's nothing wrong with him. He does everything I say at home." The school, however, defended their apparently hard-line stance, suggesting that McKenzie now needed to be dealt with by "appropriate specialists". At the time of writing, efforts were being made to find him a new school.

OPENING UP

- What is your initial response to this story? Who do you feel sympathy for?

- At what age do you think it's appropriate to expel a pupil from school? Why?

- What do you think you might have done if you were the head teacher of Sacred Heart Primary School?

DIGGING DEEPER

- Do you think exclusion is sometimes, often, or never justified? Why?

- What are some alternatives to exclusion – and do you think they can work?

- Later in life, when we behave really badly, we don't get excluded; we get imprisoned! Do you think prison can be a positive environment? Is it too harsh, or not harsh enough? Do you think we send too many people to jail, or too few?

TAKING IT TO THE WORD

Read Proverbs 22:15, and Ephesians 6:1–4

- The first verse seems to advocate corporal punishment! Do you think it does? What are your views on this?

- Taking a wider understanding of "fathers and mothers" to include the community involved in raising a child, what does Ephesians 6 have to say about this story?

- How do these two verses fit together? Do they?

- How do you think the church can get involved in the lives of children like McKenzie? Could yours?

A25

THEME: **Luck**

BIBLE: **John 10**

The bad shepherd

He's become a local celebrity in Croatia – and not only because he's the only black shepherd in the country. Accident-prone Philimon Zandamela has become a media sensation, after moving from his native Mozambique to tend flocks in the Balkans and wandering into scrape after hapless scrape.

First Philimon survived accidentally drinking sulphuric acid, then – after a fortune-teller told him it was time to die – he stabbed himself in the stomach and somehow lived to tell the tale. A string of further brushes with danger – including falling off his moped, and into a manhole, ensued, turning him into something of a national celebrity.

Many wondered whether Philimon's luck would finally run out, however, when it emerged that he and his sheep had wandered into a live minefield. Fortunately, Philimon realized what the "bumps" in the ground around him were before he or any of his sheep were blown to kingdom come. Showing uncharacteristic wisdom, he called emergency rescue services in nearby Sibenik, who led the shepherd and his flock out of the danger zone.

"I was walking along and I saw lots of strange bumps in the ground and suddenly realized where I was," Philimon later explained to the TV cameras, which again descended on his life. "Luckily, I had a mobile phone with me and could call the emergency services for help. I am very lucky to still be in one piece."

OPENING UP

- How good a shepherd do you think Philimon is? What do the sheep need from him?

- Why do you think Philimon tried to kill himself on the words of a fortune-teller? Why might some of his other brushes with death have influenced that suicide attempt?

- Why do you think Philimon has become a popular household name (and TV star) in Croatia?

DIGGING DEEPER

- Why do you think some people are so "unlucky"? Are they born that way, or somehow become so?

- Do you believe in luck? Do you think you are a lucky or unlucky person?

- Why do you think people trust fortune-tellers, psychics, or just the idea of good or bad luck?

TAKING IT TO THE WORD

Read John 10:11–18

- What is Jesus really talking about here? (Hint: it's not actually sheep!)

- What do you know about shepherds? What do you think makes a good one? Why do you think Jesus chooses to use this image to describe his relationship to us?

- How can we completely trust Jesus in a way we can't trust any human leader? What does that mean for the way you live your life?

SECTION B:
Inspiring individuals

Introduction

We all need role models. Growing up, mine included the England footballer Gary Lineker, the fictional space adventurer Han Solo, and my granddad, Fred. Three very different men, but all exceptional in their own way, and worth looking up to.

In all three cases, the thing I admired was character. Gary was a brilliant goal-scorer, but it was his attitude – on and off the pitch – which really struck me as a young lad. He epitomized fair play, almost making it through his entire career without a single moment of trouble with a referee; yet, he still managed to be the best player in every team he turned out for. Integrity became a virtue that, even at a young age, I always aspired to – and it was partly down to Gary.

In Han's case it was less clear-cut. On the face of things he was arrogant, selfish, and motivated only by money. But over the course of the *Star Wars* saga, we learned that he was actually loyal, courageous, and heroic. The refining fires of adversity brought out the real Han Solo, and that's who I decided I wanted to be – the man who "comes good" under pressure.

Fred, meanwhile, helped to shape me at far closer quarters. He never had any money in his entire life (and that which he did have disappeared quickly in pint-sized amber measures), but he worked hard every day until he died and he found contentment in it. He approached everything – death included – with a joke and a smile, and I learned incalculably from watching his example.

Three very different men, united by one thing – character. Each had character traits that were admirable and deserving of emulation. This next collection of 25 discussion starters focuses around that theme, with the stories of real men and women who have displayed real character, often in the face of adversity. None of them are perfect – in many cases they may seem very far from it – but each has something to teach us.

Arguably, of course, we should just be focusing on the characteristics of God, incarnated in his son Jesus Christ, and in many of the discussions, that's invariably where we will end up. Yet, I would suggest that each of these created individuals, knitted together by God, are able to reflect the characteristics of Christ, the gifts of the Spirit, and the heart of the Father in a small way that is both honouring to him and relatable to young people.

I certainly don't intend to pander to the celebrity culture, and I urge you to challenge this with young people whenever it arises. Yet, in the stories of real people in the public eye, we can find points of engagement and interest that can capture the interest of young people, and point away from a culture of vacuous excess, towards a Christ-like walk of character.

Like those in the first section, these stories are perhaps the ones which lend themselves best to the school context, to open youth clubs and to pre-evangelistic or evangelistic discussions. Use as many or as few of the questions as you think are appropriate, and don't forget to allow yourself the opportunity to be inspired too – both through these incredible stories and the potential-filled young people you tell them to.

B1

THEME: **Courage**

BIBLE: **Joshua 1**

Soul surfer

At age 13, Hawaiian surfer Bethany Hamilton literally had the world at her feet. She was one of the biggest talents in women's surfing, even at that tender age, and held sponsorship deals with leading companies including Rip Curl.

Then, in October 2003, tragedy struck. While surfing with friends off the coast of Kauai, Bethany was attacked by a 14-foot tiger shark. The attack left Bethany, who was lying flat on her board at the time, with a severed left arm. Her quick-thinking friends showed remarkable bravery as they worked to stop the bleeding and drag her back to shore, and while Bethany lost over 60 per cent of her blood, the quick-responding emergency crew managed to save her life.

Bethany's convalescence was marked by her unswerving positivity. Far from being downbeat, she saw this as an opportunity to tell national media about her strong Christian faith, and to declare her intention to return to surfing – competing against able-bodied surfers with only one arm.

That's exactly what she did. And in January 2009, Bethany competed in the World Junior Women's Surfing

Championships – and took second place. She now has a genuine chance of earning a place on the main women's surfing tour. Bethany credits God with her miraculous sporting recovery; one which no one had thought possible. "It was what God had taught me growing up that helped me overcome my fears to get back into the water," she says.

A film version of Bethany's life is now in production.

OPENING UP

- How do you think Bethany felt about surfing directly after her attack?

- How easy/difficult do you think it would have been to get back into the water? Why?

- Why do you believe she has been able to triumph over the odds in this way?

- Where do you think Bethany's God was in this story?

DIGGING DEEPER

- If comfortable doing so, talk about a difficult life experience or tragedy that you, or someone close to you, has faced.

- How did you/they try to overcome, work through, and move past that issue?

- What role can faith play in these kinds of circumstances? Does it offer false hope, genuine comfort, or something else?

TAKING IT TO THE WORD

Read Joshua 1:1–9

- What is the theme of God's commands to Joshua here?

- What is the connection between obeying God's teaching, and success?

- How do you think Bethany drew strength from this passage (she credits it as a favourite)?

- How could you be more brave and courageous in your Christian faith?

B2

THEME: **Life and death**

R.I.P. Jade

Throughout her relatively short adult life, Jade Goody was never far from the national media spotlight. At 20, she was thrust into the public eye as one of the most outrageous contestants ever to set foot in the *Big Brother* house, earning instant fame for her alcohol-fuelled antics. Viewers of the reality TV show either loved or hated her, like Marmite – but both groups watched on, transfixed by her ability to mispronounce words, lose her clothes, and generally make a fool of herself.

After leaving the house, the now hugely popular Jade realized that her life would never be the same, and instantly learned – and sometimes misjudged – how to manipulate the media. She became the UK's first pure celebrity: a woman who was famous simply for being famous.

The continuous media coverage of Jade's life began to resemble *The Truman Show*, and it wasn't always positive. In 2007, when she appeared in *Celebrity Big Brother*, she made a terrible error of judgment when making racist remarks about fellow contestant Shilpa Shetty. This time when she left the house, she found she had become "Public Enemy No.1".

However, when Jade was diagnosed with

terminal cancer, aged just 27, public opinion swung overwhelmingly back in her favour. Throughout her final days the media swarmed around her, as Jade weakened, married her roguish fiancé, found religion, and said goodbye to her two young children. It was as if she was the star of her own morbid soap opera – but due to the financial security it offered her boys, she willingly participated. Jade died on Mother's Day – another perfect headline for the ravenous newspapers, and a fitting end; she had died as she had lived.

- How did you feel about the way the country watched Jade die?

- Jade suffered from a difficult upbringing. Would you say that she made a success of her life? Why or why not?

- The media tried to destroy Jade after one racist comment; then made her a saint when she became ill. How do you feel about the media in the light of this?

- Think of some of the choices Jade made in her rollercoaster life. Do you think they were good or bad?

- Are you inspired by the Jade story, or does it serve as a warning? Explain your answer.

- What do you think about Jade's late conversion to Christianity? Do you think it was because she was dying? Does that matter?

- Why do you think so many people became obsessed with Jade's illness? Could it be because they find death difficult to talk about?

- How can we offer hope to people who fear death? (John 3:16 might help!)

Tracy 20/1/13

B3

THEME: **Generosity**

BIBLE: **Proverbs 11**

Increddie-Eddie

For most of us, just the idea of running a marathon is enough to make us feel tired. Twenty-six miles is more than many people run in a year, let alone in one gruelling go.

This makes the achievement of comedian and fundraiser Eddie Izzard all the more remarkable. Eddie wanted to raise funds for the charity Sport Relief, which (as part of parent charity, Comic Relief) has the bold aim of trying to eradicate poverty worldwide. Eddie knew that simply running a marathon wasn't enough to capture the public's imagination, however, so he decided not to run just one, but to run an incredible forty-three of them – in fifty-one days.

Even more extraordinarily, Eddie has never been an athlete. In fact, he's well known for being slightly overweight. Yet, for seven straight weeks, Eddie ran at least 27 miles a day, six days a week. That amounted to just over 1,100 miles across the United Kingdom! When he started, the daily distance was taking him over ten hours to complete; by the end, he had got that down to a little over five.

Eddie's incredible endurance was helped by ice

baths every evening, and despite seeing blisters pop and toenails fall off, he was determined to carry on every day, even when he was barely able to walk.

Struck by Eddie's immense effort, over 750,000 people followed his daily updates on social networking site Twitter. By the time he had finished, he had raised over £200,000 for charity, with much more money expected to pour in at a later date.

OPENING UP

- How do you feel about the idea of running a marathon?

- How about forty-three of them? Could you even imagine that was possible?

- Why do you think Eddie Izzard decided to put himself through so much pain?

- What do you think drove him to keep going when his toenails were falling off, and he could barely move?

- Why do you think he didn't just decide to give £200,000 out of his own personal wealth?

DIGGING DEEPER

- What does the word "generosity" mean to you? When do you usually use that word?

- In what other ways can we be generous, apart from with our money?

- What are some of the things you find it hard to be generous with? What do you find easier?

- How is Eddie's story an example of awesome generosity?

TAKING IT TO THE WORD

Read Proverbs 11:24–25

- The Bible contains countless verses about generosity. Why do you think it's mentioned so many times?

- What do these verses tell us are a good reason for being generous?

- Do you think these verses just apply to money? If not, what else?

- How can you become a more generous person – to the same extraordinary extent that Eddie Izzard was generous, with his time, and with the punishment he put his body through?

B4

THEME: **Ambition**

BIBLE: **Romans 15**

Kal's career

Considering how hard it is to make it as an actor in Hollywood, you would be forgiven for thinking that Kal Penn had lost his mind. The Indian–American actor, who made his name as Kumar Pater in the drug-obsessed *Harold and Kumar* movies, had hit the big time with roles in *Superman Returns, Epic Movie,* and the hit TV show *House*. Then, just as he was becoming a household name in the USA, he quit acting, had his *House* character killed off, and embarked on a completely new career.

Kal's new employer was quite a well-known man – US President Barack Obama. Having campaigned hard for Obama in the US elections the previous year, Kal agreed to take up a position working in the White House as part of President Obama's Administration.

His role, Associate Director in the Office of Public Liaison, was neither well paid nor particularly influential. Yet, Kal jumped at the chance to get into politics. In his job, he explains, he does "outreach with the American public and different organizations. It's basically the front door of the White House."

Many people have speculated that Kal will not be in a relatively low-rung position for very long. And considering that former President Ronald Reagan was once an actor, who knows where his political ambitions might end?

OPENING UP

- Which job appeals to you more – politician or movie star? Why?

- Why do you think Kal Penn chose to leave such a glamorous and well-paid career to move into politics?

- Kal has done more in thirty-two years than many people do in a lifetime – what does that tell us about his character?

DIGGING DEEPER

- How ambitious would you say you are?

- What are some of the positives and negatives of ambition?

- How can we channel and keep a check on ambition to make it more positive?

TAKING IT TO THE WORD

Read Romans 15:17–20

- How does Paul – like Kal Penn – want to serve a greater good?

- How do both these men demonstrate a positive kind of ambition?

- What about Paul's ambition is especially inspiring (verse 20)? How could we adopt this size of vision for our own communities and countries?

B5

THEME:　**Domestic violence**

BIBLE:　**Ephesians 5**

Reese's peace for women

Some celebrities use their fame to get free stuff; others to negotiate better contracts. A few, however, choose to employ the power of their celebrity to campaign for change, and to bring about justice. Bono is one famous example, but another is Reese Witherspoon, the actress and star of films such as *Legally Blonde* and *Four Christmases.*

Reese has become a campaigner around the issue of domestic violence, and has spearheaded various national and international efforts to raise awareness about it. As a young woman, Reese saw a close friend's life devastated by the effects of violence from a partner, and knew first-hand how "intimidated and ashamed" a victim can feel.

She called the problem "a pandemic" – but it's a silent one. Surveys reveal that 92 per cent of people believe they know no one who has suffered from domestic violence, despite the fact that one in four women will face it in their lifetime.

As she delivered a campaign to the UK government, calling on them to provide more funding for domestic violence support services, Reese outlined her advice to young women who could be suffering in silence. "You're not alone, and if you reach out there's somebody next door to you in your life who is ready to give you support and care and love."

The Chief Executive of Refuge, the charity which Reese was supporting, said "domestic violence affects people from all walks of life... all races, all classes, all religions. It could be your sister, your mother, your next-door neighbour. It could be your best friend."

OPENING UP

- How big a problem do you think domestic violence is in your community?

- Why do you think there was such a lack of awareness about domestic violence in the survey?

- Reese Witherspoon has used her influence on this issue – how might you, your youth leader, your church leaders and others use yours?

DIGGING DEEPER

- Why do you think domestic violence is so common? What are some of the factors that might cause or exacerbate it?

- Why do you think so many people suffer in silence?

- It's not just a male on female crime – why do you think we hear so little of male victims of domestic violence?

- Do you believe Reese Witherspoon's promise that there is always "somebody next door to you in your life" who will be ready if a victim cries for help?

TAKING IT TO THE WORD

Read Genesis 2:24 and Ephesians 5:29

- These two verses come from opposite ends of the Bible – when put together, what do they tell us is a biblical perspective on violence within marriage?

- More positively, what does the second verse mean by "as Christ does the church"? How does Christ love the church and how can we behave in the same way in our human relationships?

- Why do you think some Christians don't live this out in practice?

- How can you practically help to stand against domestic violence, and stand with its victims?

B6

THEME: **Character**

BIBLE: **Philippians 3**

Running for her life

No one could ever have predicted that Tegla Loroupe would go on to live a life of such significance. Born in Kenya in 1973, she was one of twenty-five children from her father's four wives. Growing up, she worked hard in the fields and acted as a mother to her many younger siblings. But at seven, she had the opportunity to go to school. That changed everything, but not for the reason you might expect.

Tegla's school was ten kilometres from home. Every day, she made the long journey barefoot. Such was the distance, she decided to run all the way, there and back. It was this daily journey that changed the course of her life.

Tegla quickly showed promise as a runner – after all, she was getting far more practice than anyone else! In races at school, she was beating children who were several years older than her. However, though she became determined to become an athlete, no one except her mother showed any support for the idea. Everyone else thought she was wasting her time.

Even the national athletics federation didn't support her, on the basis that she was too thin. However, after winning a prestigious cross-country race, she was nominated for the world junior athletics championships, and despite little formal training, finished 28th. At last she was recognized as having real potential, and others began to invest in her.

In 1994, Tegla ran her first marathon, in New York. She won. Fifteen years later she had won marathons all over the world, had broken a string of world records, and was the holder of records over 20, 25 and 30 kilometres. Running to school can pay off.

OPENING UP

- What characteristics did Tegla need to achieve what she did?

- How do you think Tegla felt when she wasn't supported in her quest to become an athlete?

- Do you think the opposition she faced helped her in some ways? If so, how?

DIGGING DEEPER

- What is "character"?

- What are some characteristics you might describe as positive? What about not so positive ones?

- What kind of character would you like to develop? How might you go about that?

TAKING IT TO THE WORD

Read Philippians 3:12–21

- These verses refer to running, but how is this running metaphor used to talk about the character of a Christian? (Look also at 1 Corinthians 9:24–27.)

- What kind of character does Paul want to develop – and therefore want us to develop?

- Why is it important that Jesus transforms us? Do you think we could truly change without him?

- Pray together, that God will continue to transform your character to be more like his Son.

B7

THEME: **Money**

BIBLE: **Mark 10**

A giving heart

It's becoming more common for generous individuals to give money away to those in need after they die. So-called "legacy giving" is increasingly popular, with stunned families often discovering that the fortune they thought they were inheriting from that batty aunt who died has actually been left to the local cat sanctuary.

That was also the decision made by Paul Newman, the legendary actor who later in life turned his hand to making condiments. He died in 2008, but before he did so, he made sure that his will would release an incredible $20 million to a variety of charities focused on health, the environment, education and more (although sadly, no cat sanctuaries).

The gesture catapulted Newman to the head of America's "Giving Back 30" list of generous givers in 2008. The actor headed a list which also included actors Angelina Jolie and Brad Pitt ($13.5 million), director Mel Gibson ($6 million) and boxer Oscar de la Hoya ($9.5 million). The list was compiled by the Giving Back Fund, which double-checks the claims of individuals and their publicists against tax records to ensure they are being truthful about their giving.

Paul Newman may no longer be alive, but he has left a remarkable "legacy" behind. A string of great movie performances will be enjoyed for generations; and a popular line of vinaigrettes will continue. Most crucially though, Newman knew the truth of the adage "you can't take it with you", so left his money to work hard for others long after he was gone.

OPENING UP

- Why do you think Paul Newman left so much money to people other than his family?

- How do you think his generosity will affect the way he is viewed by future generations? Will it make a difference?

- What motivates people to give money away? Why do some people find it so hard?

DIGGING DEEPER

- Do you dream of being wealthy? Why or why not?

- If you became wealthy, how generous do you imagine you might be?

- Why do you think many rich people aren't as generous as you might expect?

- How easy do you think it is to fall in love with money?

TAKING IT TO THE WORD

Read Mark 10:17–31

- What do you make of Jesus' incredible statement to the rich man? Is he being literal?

- Why is it so hard for rich people to follow God with all their hearts?

- What does it mean for the last to be first and vice versa? How should that effect the way we view money and possessions?

B8

THEME: **Activism/slavery**

BIBLE: **Luke 4**

Teenage revolutionary

Most 12-year-olds find their lives are pretty full. A combination of chasing the newly discovered opposite sex, trying not to act like a child and worrying about acne is usually enough to keep even the most energetic pre-teen busy. Not always though. When Zach Hunter was 12, he founded an international anti-slavery campaign.

Zach was a fairly ordinary American boy, a fan of music, reading, and playing tennis. He struggled with shyness, and hated speaking in public. But when his mother told him about the plight of the estimated 27 million slaves in the world today, Zach's reaction was to start to rally others to change that fact.

In the same year, Zach founded his own charity – "Loose Change to Loosen Chains". He claimed to have worked out that Americans had around $10 billion of loose change simply hanging around in their houses. He came up with a simple yellow collecting cup, got some friends to rattle them around their school, and raised $6,000 in two weeks. From there, the charity rapidly expanded, and Zach soon became directly involved in liberating people from slavery all over the world, through his support of charities such as International

Justice Mission.

Today Zach is an international speaker (his school principal sees it as "like being a travelling athlete") and the author of several books on slavery and activism. He encourages young people all over the US and beyond to "be the change" they want to see in the world. His age appears to be irrelevant – he is a true revolutionary, propelled by his faith in Jesus to see his world change for the better.

OPENING UP

- What does it mean to "be the change"? Is that a realistic rallying cry?

- What kind of opposition do you think Zach has faced? Why do you think he's managed to create a movement?

- Do you think any teenager could do something like this, or does it take a specially "gifted" person?

DIGGING DEEPER

- What do you know about modern slavery? Where do you think it still occurs?

- How could you or your community have links to slavery? How could you find out?

- What can we do practically to join the fight against slavery?

TAKING IT TO THE WORD

Read Luke 4:18–19 and John 14:12

- Jesus begins his ministry with these words recorded in Luke, directly quoted from Isaiah 61:1–2. What kind of things did Jesus come to do?

- What do Jesus' words in John 14:12 then suggest about this mission?

- What is Jesus saying directly about slavery here?

- Having read these verses, do you think Jesus wants us to be activists in our world? Why or why not?

B9

THEME:　**Perseverance/disability**

BIBLE:　**James 1**

Life without limbs

As a child, Nick Vujicic always inspired looks of compassion and pity from everyone around him. The firstborn son of an Australian pastor, Nick's birth was a bittersweet moment, as he entered the world without any arms or legs. His parents had received no warning that this was the case; the first they knew of these devastating disabilities was at his birth.

Understandably, on the day in 1982, Nick's parents and their church were devastated. They wrestled with the question of why a God of love could allow something like this to happen – especially to a family of his followers. The Bible verse to "consider it pure joy... whenever you face trials of many kinds" seemed a particularly hard one to swallow.

A lot of pain and struggle followed – for Nick and his parents. At times, Nick confesses that he had thoughts of rejection, depression and even suicide. Yet, thanks to his supportive family, and his growing faith in God, Nick made it through his teenage years, and even graduated from university with a finance degree.

Today, Nick is an internationally renowned motivational speaker, travelling all over the world to share the story of his triumph over adversity. It doesn't stop there though – Nick uses the platform created by his disability to share his passion for the story of Jesus Christ. Coming from someone who has had to struggle and persevere so much – and yet, still retains a vibrant faith – his words are somehow more powerful than those of a perma-tanned TV evangelist. In spite of what his parents feared at his birth, Nick Vujicic is making a huge impact on the world.

OPENING UP

- We take our limbs for granted. Could you imagine life without them? How would you function?

- Why do you think Nick didn't simply give up on life?

- Why do you think Nick's words have such an impact when he gets on to a platform and talks about his Christian faith?

DIGGING DEEPER

- How do you think society views people with disabilities?

- How do you feel about the way in which many pregnancies are terminated when "abnormalities" are discovered? Is this right?

- What's your reaction to people with disabilities? Do you interact regularly with anyone like this?

TAKING IT TO THE WORD

Read James 1:2–12

- How can James realistically expect people to be thankful for trouble and trial?

- What is perseverance, and why is it so important?

- Do you do what James suggests in verse 5 when you are struggling? Why or why not?

- How do James' words in verses 9–12 offer encouragement and hope to people like Nick Vujicic?

B10

THEME: **Dreams**

BIBLE: **Luke 18**

How to achieve your childhood dreams

In late 2006, American professor Randy Pausch was diagnosed with pancreatic cancer. Like anyone receiving such a diagnosis, his world fell apart in an instant. Worse still, the following summer, Randy was told that he had around three months left to live. Most of us know that we wouldn't react to such news with anything other than despair. Randy, however, had a different reaction.

Randy realized that he had an educational legacy to leave. He began work on a final lecture, based on the idea that all professors want to give a "last lecture" summing up all they have learned in their careers. Randy's lecture was entitled "Really achieving your childhood dreams", and catalogued Randy's journey to fulfil six dreams he had had since a child. When he gave it at Carnegie Mellon University, there was only standing room available in the 450-capacity lecture theatre.

On the whole, Randy's journey had been a successful one. He got to experience being in zero gravity after impersonating a journalist at NASA; got an article published in the *World Book Encyclopaedia*; met the actor who played Captain Kirk in *Star Trek*; worked for Disney, and even "became one of those guys who wins stuffed animals at funfairs". Randy's only failure was in the most unlikely area – becoming an NFL footballer – and he was happy to concede that some things simply aren't possible for everyone.

Randy's speech wasn't finished there, however. In the second part, he went on to talk about his life's work as a professor: enabling the dreams of others. He gave a number of examples of how he had sought to inspire his students, but one was particularly striking: the story of one of his students, who held a dream of working on a *Star Wars* film. Thanks partly to Randy's belief in him, that student went on to work for Lucasfilm, and was on the crew of all three *Star Wars* prequels.

Randy died in 2008, but his legacy remains. A book, based on his last lecture, was still on the *New York Times* best-sellers list over a year and a half after its author's death.

OPENING UP

- What were some of your childhood dreams? Did you achieve any of them?

- What characteristics must Randy have had to enable him to achieve his?

- Why do you think his lecture and book attracted so many people?

DIGGING DEEPER

- What are your hopes and dreams for the next five years of your life?

- What about in the long-term? Do you have any big dreams for the rest of your life? (Please share them – however embarrassing that might seem.)

- How does it feel to share your dreams out loud with others?

- How could you practically take inspiration from Randy Pausch as you look to achieve them?

TAKING IT TO THE WORD

Read Luke 18:1–8

- What was the widow's dream and how did she achieve it?

- How could this story also apply to our lives and dreams?

- What is the final question about? Why is this important to us when we consider our dreams?

B11

THEME: **Conservation**

BIBLE: **Genesis 2**

Ahead of her time

When most people think of Beatrix Potter, they think of fluffy animals with painfully cute names like Flopsy and Tiggywinkle. That's hardly surprising, since she remains one of the most popular children's authors of all time, over fifty years after her death. Yet, Potter is now also remembered as a remarkable conservationist, who took practical steps to protect her beloved countryside long before the rest of the world saw the need.

As a child, Beatrix and her brother would spend long summers in Scotland and the Lake District of England, where she developed a love of wildlife that would one day form the basis for her writing. At the other end of her life, after she had become a successful author, she moved to the country and began buying up more and more farmland, where she reared sheep, met and married a local man, and became increasingly involved in campaigning for the preservation of the countryside.

When she died, Beatrix Potter left over 4,000 acres of land to the English National Trust, meaning that it would be preserved for generations of people to enjoy. Even when she did this, no one realized how important a gesture she was making.

Her farms are today enjoyed by thousands of visitors each year, and her gift remains one of the biggest legacies ever made.

OPENING UP

- Why do you think Beatrix Potter was so passionate about the countryside at a time when others were more short-sighted about conservation?

- Do you find the countryside boring or inspiring? Why?

- Could Beatrix have made better use of her wealth?

DIGGING DEEPER

- How important is conservation to you?

- With the world population growing, do you think we should be more or less concerned about saving areas of countryside?

- Do you think we should try to save endangered species, or should we simply subscribe to the idea of the "survival of the fittest"?

- How can you practically help to look after the planet?

TAKING IT TO THE WORD

Read Genesis 2:4–20 (you could omit verses 10–14)

- God created the Earth as a lush and incredibly varied place. Why do you think he did this?

- What is man's role in regard to the Earth? To what degree do we still do this today?

- Why do you think Adam was given the role of naming the animals? What does that tell us about how God sees us in relation to nature?

B12

THEME: **Entrepreneurship**

BIBLE: **1 Corinthians 9**

Making his Mark

At age 25, he was worth $2 billion. He may be the most famous person you couldn't pick out of a crowd. And apparently, his success was mainly down to luck. By any accounts, Mark Zuckerberg is an extraordinary man.

A computer programmer from a young age, Mark was the founder and inventor of Facebook, a web-based program which he designed while at Harvard University. Before he had even done that, however, he had already designed Synapse, a music player which used artificial intelligence to learn the user's taste in music. AOL and Microsoft tried to recruit Mark while he was still a teenager, but he chose instead to attend Harvard. As it turned out, this was a wise move.

In early 2004, Mark launched Facebook from his college room. It was intended as an online version of the student directory (often known as a "face-book") which would solely be for Harvard. However, following the advice of a friend, Mark allowed the system to spread to several other schools. Within two years, Facebook was spreading like wildfire. In early 2010, there were around 350 million users worldwide.

OPENING UP

- Why do you think Facebook was so successful?

- How do you feel when you hear about people who have been successful at such a young age? Do you feel jealous or inspired?

- Why do you think Mark turned down AOL and Microsoft as a teenager? Do you think you could do that?

DIGGING DEEPER

- What is an entrepreneur?

- Does an entrepreneur just have to be concerned about making money? Or can you be a different kind of entrepreneur?

- How could you be entrepreneurial in your community? How could this approach change things for the better?

TAKING IT TO THE WORD

Read 1 Corinthians 9:19–23

- What does Paul mean when he says he is "all things to all men"? How might this be misinterpreted?

- How can you be like Paul in attempting to understand your "target market" for the gospel – your local community?

- Should we be as obsessive as Paul (he makes himself "a slave")? Or could that be unhealthy?

B13

THEME: **Patience**

BIBLE: **1 Samuel 16**

Nelson's wait

Nelson Mandela is one of the most famous men on the planet, and one of the few people certain to become a feature in the history books (or at least, online learning communities!) of the future. He is the man credited with leading South Africa out of the Apartheid era, one of the most charismatic men ever to walk the earth, and a global statesman.

Before he was able to accomplish many of his achievements, however, Mandela was forced to wait. As a prisoner on the now infamous Robben Island, he spent many of his 27 years of incarceration living in the most basic surroundings. For long periods, his life there consisted of hard labour in a lime quarry. Even though he possessed fabulous gifts of leadership, he remained in the prison, waiting, watching the supposedly best years of his life waste away before his eyes.

Mandela was eventually released from prison in 1990. In the years that followed, he became a global figurehead for racial equality – arguably blazing a trail for others including Barack Obama to follow. He was part of a successful campaign to create a multi-racial election system that didn't favour whites, and benefited personally when in 1994 he was elected as South Africa's President.

Even when his political career came to an end, Mandela wasn't finished. He chose the occasion of his 89th birthday to announce the formation of a new global leadership network called "The Elders". The group, chaired by Archbishop Desmond Tutu, brings leaders together to discuss solutions to some of the world's biggest problems. Though his chance to be truly influential came late in life, Mandela grabbed it with both hands.

OPENING UP

- What to you are some of the most inspiring elements of Nelson Mandela's story?

- How do you think Mandela was able to endure 27 years of prison and still come out with an appetite to change the world?

- Can you imagine being imprisoned for 27 years? How might it change you?

DIGGING DEEPER

- Are you good or bad at waiting? Give a recent example of when you had to wait for something.

- In what ways/areas are you used to waiting for things?

- When and how can waiting be a good thing?

- When does it feel most frustrating and negative?

TAKING IT TO THE WORD

Read 1 Samuel 16:11–23

- What happened after God "anointed" David as his king? Did he become king straight away?

- How do you think it felt for David to have to remain a shepherd, then become a warrior, before eventually being crowned king?

- Why do you think God took him on this long journey?

- David's patience – he returns to his sheep even though he will be king – is inspiring. How can we learn from his example as we seek to learn patience?

B14

THEME: **Kindness**

BIBLE: **Matthew 7**

Offensive kindness

Benny, David and James were three friends with a shared passion – kindness. In 2008, they formed a movement called "The Kindness Offensive" (TKO), a community initiative which quickly became known for bestowing random acts of kindness on members of the public. TKO started when the three friends travelled to London's Parliament Hill to ask the public what kind of kindness they would like to receive.

Over the months that followed, TKO gave away hundreds of gig and sports tickets, food, kitchen equipment, handmade chocolates and more. In October 2008, they gave away 25 tonnes of non-perishable food to various centres of need, including the Salvation Army. As momentum grew around them, so their ideas got even bigger: in February 2009 they gave away over 500,000 pancakes.

Today the influence of TKO continues to grow rapidly. Their rallying cry is "practise random kindness and senseless acts of beauty", a phrase borrowed from the writer Anne Herbert. They have captured the imagination of thousands of Londoners and the movement shows no sign of slowing.

OPENING UP

- What do you think drives the members of The Kindness Offensive to do what they do?

- What kind of reactions do you think the members of TKO get when they are "randomly kind"?

- What do you think the phrase "senseless acts of beauty" means?

DIGGING DEEPER

- How does it feel to be really kind to someone?

- How does it feel when someone is really kind to you? What effect does it have on you?

- Can kindness change the way a community feels? If so, how?

- Are there any drawbacks to kindness?

TAKING IT TO THE WORD

Read Matthew 7:12

- This verse is known as "the golden rule" – why?

- In an ideal world, how would you like others to treat you?

- Is that realistic though? Could you really begin to treat others in the way that you would like to be treated?

- How do random acts of kindness help us to answer Jesus' command here?

- Think of at least one random act of kindness that you could perform in your community this week.

B15

THEME: **Responding to need**

BIBLE: **Isaiah 1**

An amazing wind-up

Trevor Baylis is the most inspiring kind of inventor, because his passion to innovate wasn't driven by a love of money, but by a desire to help people.

In 1989, Trevor was at home watching a television programme about the HIV/AIDS pandemic. The programme suggested that the spread of the disease in Africa could be significantly slowed down by the introduction of educational initiatives, and sending information through radio broadcasts. Before the programme had even finished airing, Trevor was in his workshop assembling his response.

Trevor's big idea was the wind-up radio – and his prototype consisted of parts from a toy car, transistor radio, and music box. When he tried to take the idea to production, however, he found that he was met with widespread rejection. No one could see the potential for the idea – especially because the target audience were poverty-stricken Africans.

For five years Trevor found no backer for his idea, but in 1994 a television appearance finally attracted some investors. By 1997, he had created an even better version of the radio, which could run for an hour on twenty seconds of winding, and put it into mass production. The impact in Africa, where public health broadcasts can now take vital information into the farthest reaches of the continent, has been incalculable.

OPENING UP

- Artists are generally more celebrated than inventors. Why do you think this is?

- Why do you think Trevor had such difficulty getting support for his wind-up radio?

DIGGING DEEPER

- What kind of "need" do you see around you in your community? Who is struggling?

- How do you feel about this need? Do you feel powerful or powerless to respond?

- How are people in your community already responding to those needs? If you were to adopt a Trevor Baylis approach, how could you innovate to meet needs in your community?

TAKING IT TO THE WORD

Read Isaiah 1:16–17 (you could also read the rest of the chapter as context)

- What does it mean to "seek justice"?

- Do these verses suggest that we should be reactive or proactive in responding to need? Why?

- Pray together for the needs in your community – that God might inspire you to respond to them in his name.

B16

THEME: **Forgiveness**

BIBLE: **Matthew 5**

Remarkable forgiveness

Corrie Ten Boom wasn't Jewish, but her remarkable acts of courage and kindness towards Jews during the Second World War still saw her end up inside the walls of a Nazi death camp. Corrie, a Dutch watchmaker and youth worker, earned her place in the infamous Ravensbrück concentration camp by harbouring Jewish refugees in her home in the early 1940s.

Corrie's family, devout Christians who believed that the Jews had a special place in God's heart, built a secret hiding place in Corrie's room which was able to hold many people. It was specially constructed in order to fool the Nazis responsible for hunting Jews, so that the walls did not sound hollow. Thanks to the ingenious construction of the hiding place, it was never found by the SS.

The Ten Boom family were eventually arrested though, and imprisoned, first at Scheveningen Prison, where her father died soon after his capture. While most of her family were then released, Corrie and her sister Betsie were sent to another camp, and finally to Ravensbrück. Eventually, Betsie also died.

On New Years Eve 1944, Corrie was released. A

week later, after the rest of the women her age in the camp were executed, Corrie learned that her release had been granted by mistake, due to an administrative error. In response, she said simply: "God does not have problems; only plans."

In 1947, Corrie was faced with a true test of her faith, however. A former guard from Ravensbrück, one of the cruellest men in the camp, approached Corrie to ask for her forgiveness. In her book, *Tramp for the Lord*, she admitted that she had found this hard, but prayed to God for the strength to forgive. She explained: "for a long moment we grasped each other's hands, the former guard and the former prisoner. I had never known God's love so intensely as I did then."

OPENING UP

- What do you make of Corrie's words? How could she feel God's love when faced with a man who had abused her so terribly?

- What are some of the most remarkable elements in this story? How do they make you feel?

- How do you think Corrie kept her faith when all this was happening to her?

DIGGING DEEPER

- How easy or difficult do you find it to forgive? When is it harder or easier?

- Is it important to forgive people who wrong you, or is it better sometimes to remember?

- Why can forgiveness sometimes feel too hard? How do we deal with that?

- What are some of the consequences of not forgiving?

TAKING IT TO THE WORD

Read Matthew 5:21–26

- Who is Jesus suggesting is our "brother" in verse 23? What implications do these verses have for our worship?

- Why does Jesus suggest we should settle matters even with our enemies before we reach court?

- In Luke 6:35, Jesus says we should "love our enemies" and even lend money to them without expecting it back! How easy or difficult is this? Why is Jesus suggesting it?

B17

THEME: **Turning around**

BIBLE: **Acts 9**

Out of the fire

Nicky Cruz was one of seventeen children, born into a Satanist family in Puerto Rico in 1938. At home, his parents brutally abused him, both physically and mentally, and when he wasn't being abused, he was being neglected. As a teenager, he was sent to New York to live with his brother, but in rebellion to his parents decided to go it alone on the streets of the city.

Within a few days, Nicky had suffered a gang beating so bad it left him unable to move for more than a week. Rather than returning to his brother, however, Nicky trained himself, improved his fighting tactics, and sought out the gang leader in order to take his revenge. He found the man, and beat him to a pulp – and in doing so sent out a message to the neighbourhood, which soon attracted interest from other gangs.

Nicky was invited to join a vicious gang named the "Mau Maus", named after the uprising in 1960s Kenya. Within six months, he had been elected Warlord of the gang, and soon after that they became notorious in the city.

Shortly afterwards, he met a Christian minister, David Wilkerson, who was preaching on the Mau Mau's "turf". David told Nicky that God loved him and would never stop doing so; Nicky slapped David and threatened to kill him. That afternoon, David defiantly appeared at the Mau Mau's headquarters to repeat his message. Again, Nicky slapped him.

When, two weeks later, Nicky heard that David would be holding an evangelistic meeting nearby, he decided to go along with other members of the gang and teach the preacher a lesson. When he arrived, however, he began to feel guilty for his life as a gangster, and started to pray. David Wilkerson prayed with him, and he asked God to forgive him.

The next day, Nicky and many of the Mau Maus handed in weapons to the police, and renounced the gang lifestyle. Nicky returned to school and became a preacher, and he returned to his old neighbourhood and began preaching to the Mau Maus. He persuaded many of them, including the gang's new leader, to become Christians too.

OPENING UP

- How difficult do you think Nicky's decision was for him? What would have been some of the consequences of what he did in the end?

- Why do you think Nicky went to the preacher's meeting?

- What impact might Nicky's conversion have had on the local community and gang culture?

DIGGING DEEPER

- Have you ever completely changed your mind on something – a favourite sports team, a political belief or a religious one? What happened?

- How easy or difficult is it to switch allegiance?

- How easy do you find it to admit that you are wrong? Why?

TAKING IT TO THE WORD

Read Acts 9:1–22

- This is a long passage but an incredible story. What impact would Saul's conversion have had on the people who heard him preaching?

- How do you think Saul felt, preaching in the synagogues about the Jesus he had once spoken against?

- A modern equivalent might be Richard Dawkins suddenly converting to Christianity. What impact might that have on today's culture? Why?

B18

THEME: **Friendship**

BIBLE: **Ecclesiastes 4**

For friendship

They were three of the most famous actors in the world, used to commanding astronomical fees for their screen performances. Yet, for Johnny Depp, Jude Law, and Colin Farrell, this movie wasn't about money. This movie was *The Imaginarium of Doctor Parnassus*, the final film of actor Heath Ledger. Ledger died midway through filming, and so in order to complete the project, director Terry Gilliam approached the three stars to request their involvement. All three agreed instantly.

Gilliam had worked with Depp on another movie which was never finished, *The Man who Killed Don Quixote*. When he got the director's call, he simply replied, "I'm in." Next he asked Law, who was originally scheduled to play Ledger's role but had to pull out due to other commitments. He also agreed on the spot.

Ledger's role had been divided into four parts by Gilliam – a move which eventually made surprising sense in the surreal world of the final film – so the director was still short of an actor. At Ledger's funeral, he spotted Farrell, and later admitted, "I didn't know he was a friend." He approached Farrell, and he too accepted the offer.

The three men's willingness to lay down their own schedules was due entirely to their great affection for their friend, who had been found dead in a New York hotel room in circumstances that have still never been explained. As a final act of memorial, they also donated their fees for the film to Ledger's infant daughter Matilda. Her mother, the actress Michelle Williams, said the three men had "behaved heroically". She added: "if anything positive has come out of this, it is to have seen good people being decent."

OPENING UP

- Why do you think the three men agreed to give up paying jobs to make this film?

- How do you think the director Terry Gilliam was affected by their responses to his request?

- How might their acts also have helped Michelle Williams and Matilda to grieve?

DIGGING DEEPER

- What is true friendship? How do you define it?

- How would it feel to lose a close friend in this way? (It may have happened to you – share only what you feel comfortable with.)

- How have you or others commemorated the deaths of close friends or family members? Why this way?

TAKING IT TO THE WORD

Read Ecclesiastes 4:8–12

- What do these verses have to say about friendship?

- Do your own friendships look like this? How have you "lifted up" your friends when they have "fallen"?

- Why does the writer describe the relationship between two people as "a cord of three strands"?

- Pray together, that you would be friends who support and catch each other in times of need.

B19

THEME: **Fashion**

BIBLE: **Matthew 23**

Dressed for success?

Robert Pattinson is a movie star who came from nowhere – the lead actor in the *Twilight* movies who was previously a complete unknown. It was a similar story for Gordon Brown, the man who stood in the shadows while Tony Blair took the glory (and the flak) for a decade before eventually becoming British Prime Minister. Now both Pattinson and Brown have something else in common – a place on *GQ* magazine's best-dressed man list.

Well, almost. Because while the infamous vampire was hailed as the world's best-dressed man by the trendy men's magazine, Mr Brown found himself at the absolute opposite end of the fashion rankings. According to *GQ*, Gordon Brown is the world's worst-dressed man.

Brown beat French President Nicolas Sarkozy, stand-up comic Russell Brand, and even military-attired Korean dictator Kim Jong-Il to the title, which presumably never graced the mantelpiece of No. 10 Downing Street. The magazine said he was "anything but a prime example of British style".

At the other end of the spectrum, Pattinson was described – by designers Dolce and Gabbana no less –

as "extremely elegant and inspiring; the true essence of a contemporary man". Having beaten the likes of David Beckham, Daniel Craig, and er, Fantastic Mr Fox to the accolade, former model Pattinson is probably assured of a few more contracts in the coming years.

OPENING UP

- Who do you think was affected more by the publication of this list? Robert Pattinson or Gordon Brown? Why?

- Do you think they were really evaluated on how they dressed? Or is there more to it?

- Do you think the judges got it right? Are there better or worse dressed people out there?

DIGGING DEEPER

- How important is fashion to you? How much of your money do you spend on clothes, and why?

- What do you think people's clothes say about them? Would you ever choose friends based on their clothes?

- How much thought do you put into how and where your clothes were made? Do you check if your clothes were made ethically?

TAKING IT TO THE WORD

Read Matthew 23:25–28

- Jesus is talking to the Pharisees here – what kind of behaviour is he criticizing?

- What does his criticism tell us about God's view of "putting on appearances"?

- How does this passage serve as a warning to the fashion-obsessed?

B20

THEME: **Humour**

BIBLE: **James 3**

Clean Tim

Some might say comedy has become more sophisticated over the years; others would argue that in an increasingly sexualized culture, toilet humour and the lowest common denominator have become king. One thing's for sure though – bad language and sexual references are meat and drink to today's stand-up comedians. Well, almost all of them.

Stand up – and step forward – Tim Vine, the British comedian who refuses to use profanity in his act, and rarely mentions sex. For more than a decade, Tim has been one of the UK's most popular comedians, with sell-out tours and top-selling live DVDs to his name. He's had one of the lead roles in one of the country's best-loved sitcoms, and has even held the Guinness World Record for most jokes told in an hour – an incredible 499.

Tim's act avoids the usual subject matter by consisting almost entirely of puns – such as "one-armed butlers: they can take it, but they can't dish it out". Bob Monkhouse, one of the most successful British comedians of all time, said Tim had "taken the trick of word play and extended it to lengths no one has ever dared before". By concentrating on this area of comedy,

Tim has managed to keep his principles intact – and has enjoyed great success as a result.

OPENING UP

- Do you think Tim is a special case because he specializes in word play, or could all comedians become clean?

- Do you imagine you would find Tim funny? Why or why not?

- If you believe in God, how do you think he views Tim's decision (Tim is a Christian) to "keep it clean"?

DIGGING DEEPER

- Why do you think so much humour is based around sex and bodily functions?

- What kind of humour do you tend to use most? What kind do you like to listen to? Why these styles?

- Where are the boundaries of comedy? When does it become offensive or unhelpful?

TAKING IT TO THE WORD

Read James 3:1–12

- What do verses 9–11 in particular have to say about our use of humour?

- Do you know anyone who is able to keep their tongue completely in check?

- Why is it so difficult to say only good, helpful, edifying things?

- How easy or difficult do you find it to think before you speak?

B21

THEME: **Doing what's right**

BIBLE: **1 Peter 2**

Blowing the whistle

Mordechai Vanunu is not a household name. Yet, his actions as a lowly engineer in Israel had an extraordinary impact on international relations at the end of the last millennium.

As a technician at the Negev Nuclear Research Center in the 1970s, Vanunu learned for certain what others only suspected – that Israel was developing nuclear weapons, in order to protect itself against the perceived threat of Arab nations. Internationally, Israel had maintained a policy of deliberate ambiguity with regard to whether it was developing the weapons, but now Vanunu – an Israeli Christian, knew the truth.

For a decade, he kept this secret to himself. But when Israel destroyed a nuclear reactor in Iraq – part of that country's nuclear weapons programme – Vanunu became uncomfortable, and took an active part in demonstrations against the military action. Then, estimating that Israel had enough plutonium to manufacture around 150 nuclear weapons, he felt he needed to go further than simply protesting.

Vanunu took his information to the newspapers in Great Britain, and in 1986, revelations about Israel's nuclear programme were published. The engineer had put himself directly in the firing line through his actions, and soon found himself in prison for treason – where he spent eleven years in solitary confinement and a further seven behind bars. Some saw him as a heroic whistle-blower, others as a traitor.

In 2004, shortly before his release, Vanunu remained defiant. In recordings which were only made public after he had been released, he said, "I am neither a traitor nor a spy. I only wanted the world to know what was happening." At time of writing, Vanunu is still not an entirely free man – he is still unable to leave Israel, and despite the assertions of Amnesty International and others that he has no case left to answer, he remains there with no guarantee of ever being allowed to leave.

OPENING UP

- Was Israel right to imprison Vanunu for all that time? Why or why not?

- Do you think, ten years into solitary imprisonment, he regretted what he had done?

- Why do you think Vanunu revealed Israel's nuclear secrets? Could he have acted differently?

DIGGING DEEPER

- What do you think you might have done in this situation?

- If you knew a member of your family had done something terrible and was trying to conceal it, what would you do?

- When is it hardest to do the right thing?

- When have you chosen to do the right thing even though it was hard? When have you chosen not to?

TAKING IT TO THE WORD

Read 1 Peter 2:13–17

- Does this passage support Israeli government, or Vanunu? Why?

- What does it mean to "not use your freedom as a cover-up for evil"?

- How can you fulfil all the commands in verse 17 if they are in opposition to each other – as in this story?

B22

THEME: **Money/talent**

BIBLE: **Luke 19**

The parable of Shakira

Shakira Isabel Mebarak Ripoli was eight years old when her father was declared bankrupt. While the details were being ironed out, Shakira was sent from her home in Colombia, South America, to live with relatives in Los Angeles. When she returned home, she was shocked to discover that most of her parents' possessions had been sold.

To demonstrate that things could have been worse, Shakira's father took her to a park in their home town, Barranquilla. There she saw teenage orphans who lived there, sniffing glue. Even at that young age, she had ambitions both to help people and to become a recording artist. She now claims that at that moment she decided to help those young people when she became a famous musician.

Displaying obvious musical talent from a young age, Shakira did win a recording contract as a teenager, but it was not until 1995, with the release of her third album *Pies Descalzos*, that she hit the big time. At 18, she was already a huge star in Spain and Latin America, and within just a few years she was also a commercial success in the English-speaking world.

Shakira didn't wait for the latter success to fulfil the promise she had made as a child. In 1995, she set up the Pies Descalzos Foundation, named after her breakthrough album. The charity, which she continues to fund today, runs special schools for underprivileged children throughout Colombia. She has subsequently helped to found more charities, and is a UNICEF Goodwill Ambassador.

The enormous success that Shakira has enjoyed has not shaken her desire to help people. While she is currently rated the fourth highest female earner in the music industry, she is also one of the busiest and most thoughtful doers of good in the world. Addressing the Oxford University Union in 2009, she even offered a convincing plea for world peace: "I want us... to send 30,000 educators to Afghanistan, not 30,000 soldiers; that world education becomes more important than world domination." Out of most mouths that might sound shallow, but Shakira has earned the right to say such things.

OPENING UP

- Is it easier for Shakira to be so generous when she has so much?

- How does Shakira's approach to wealth and celebrity differ from the norm? What might be a more usual example?

- Why do you think Shakira was taken seriously when she addressed the intellectuals of the Oxford Union?

DIGGING DEEPER

- Do you think it's easier to give when you have much or little? Why?

- What are some different kinds of generosity?

- How do you think you stay grounded when you become rich or successful?

TAKING IT TO THE WORD

Read Luke 19:11–27

- Does this story seem fair? Why or why not?

- What do you think Jesus is getting at in this parable? What's the real meaning behind it?

- Which character in this parable has Shakira been most like?

- What does this parable have to say to us?

B23

THEME: **Adventure!**

BIBLE: **2 Timothy 1**

Soul survivor

Considering he's now known as one of the world's premier action men, Bear Grylls was raised in surprisingly sedate surroundings. His dad was a politician, his mother an upper-middle-class lady affectionately known as "Lady Grylls". Of course, they didn't christen him "Bear" – that nickname came along when he was a child and just seemed to stick. His real name is Edward Michael Grylls – but he hasn't been known as that since before he was a Boy Scout.

Scouting has since become a key part of Bear's life – he began his growth as a young adventurer in that movement, and in 2009 was named Chief Scout – a prestigious ambassadorial role that makes him a role model for young people in the UK and beyond.

His years as a Scout led him naturally into a three-year stint in the British Special Forces, where he learned many of the survival skills for which he is now famous. Then, at 23, he became one of the youngest people to climb Mount Everest, and threw himself into a number of dangerous challenges, each of which both raised funds for good causes and raised his profile a little further.

Before long, Bear's obvious potential as a TV star had been spotted, and he began to make survival documentaries, first in the UK, and then in the USA. His show *Born Survivor* (known elsewhere as *Man vs Wild*) became a huge international hit with its mix of gorgeous scenery and death-defying escapades. His main focus over the proceeding years has simply been to avoid death, while risking it regularly.

Bear's life is a somewhat unusual mix of adventure, family life, celebrity stardom, and Bible study. Bear is a committed Christian – a surprising revelation for many of his fans – and speaks regularly around the world at evangelistic events. For many, he presents an intriguing picture of manliness – masculine and tough, while also being humble enough to believe in a higher God.

OPENING UP

- Do you think some people would be surprised to discover Bear's faith? Why or why not?

- What impact does it have on you that such a well-known and respected man believes passionately in Jesus? What impact might it have on others?

- Do you think Bear is being responsible taking so many risks when he has a family? Why or why not?

DIGGING DEEPER

- How do you feel about the idea of adventure? Does it excite or daunt you? Why?

- What are some different kinds of adventure that don't involve death-defying leaps and surviving on maggots?

- Do you see potential for adventure in your own life? Where?

TAKING IT TO THE WORD

Read 2 Timothy 1:3–12

- What does verse 7 tell us about God's plan for adventure in our lives?

- How else does this passage suggest the "adventure" of the Christian life?

- How do you think your Christian faith could better reflect an attitude of adventure? Pray together, that God will lead you into a deeper adventure with him.

B24

THEME: **Pushy parents**

BIBLE: **Colossians 3**

Too Young for Kirsty

British Radio presenter Kirsty Young caused a stir when she criticized pushy parents – but did she have a point?

When newsreader Kirsty hit out at parents who try to mould their children into "baby einsteins", she received a wave of criticism. She called the phenomenon of parents who push their children too hard a "modern disease", and claimed that people were simply trying to use children as an "extension of their own success".

In an article in the magazine *Radio Times*, the mother of two said children were being funnelled into areas of achievement such as extra maths classes and Chinese lessons. She described how she had been forced to question her own ability as a parent when she visited a prospective nursery school and found three-year-olds doing improvement exercises. "The idea that they're going to come home (aged 3) and show me their jotters just makes me want to puke," she wrote.

Kirsty's criticism flies in the face of a culture which encourages parents to play a "full role" in their children's education. But with statistics suggesting that schools with a high degree of parental involvement produce better results, is she right to complain?

OPENING UP

- Do you agree with Kirsty? Are some parents too involved in their children's education?

- At what age do you think homework should begin? Why?

- Why do you think some parents push their children so hard?

DIGGING DEEPER

- Would you like your parents to be more or less involved in your education? Do they ask you to do activities you would rather not – or should they support you more?

- What might be some of the positive and negative effects of pushy parents?

- What might be some of the effects – good and bad – of parents who take a back seat in their children's education?

TAKING IT TO THE WORD

Read Colossians 3:18–21

- This passage creates a picture of a loving family – how does it match up to your experience of family? (Only share as much as you are comfortable with.)

- Is it realistic to be expected to "obey your parents in everything"? Why or why not?

- What do you think the writer means when he suggests children will become discouraged if they are embittered (another translation uses "exasperate" instead of "embitter")?

- How can families work together better to make this idea work?

B25

THEME: **Sabbath**

BIBLE: **Exodus 20**

Euan says no

Euan Murray is one of the best rugby players to emerge from Scotland in recent years. Yet, when his national team lined up in a key fixture against France in March 2010, Euan wasn't on the pitch. He wasn't injured or ineligible, and his coach would have loved him to have played. Euan had declined the invitation, however – because he wasn't prepared to work on a Sunday.

In 2005, Euan suffered a serious head injury, and began a period of soul-searching which led to the rekindling of his Christian faith, which had gone off the boil during the early years of his rugby career. After returning to the game, he resolved to make his faith – rather than his sport – the focus of his life, although for several years he continued to play rugby on Sundays, usually when televised games were switched from their Saturday slots.

However, turning out for Sunday matches began to feel increasingly wrong to Euan, who felt compelled to follow the biblical command to "remember the Sabbath day". "I was going against my conscience," he later told the media, "and it became impossible to enjoy. I realised it's quite simple, really. Jesus said, 'If you love me, keep my commandments' and there are ten commandments – not nine."

He continued, "I want to excel in rugby because that's where I've been given the opportunity to serve my God – but it has to fit with the way I want to live my life... I want to live my life believing and doing the things he wants and the Sabbath day is a full day. It's not a case of a couple of hours in church then playing rugby or going down the pub; it's the full day."

A clause in Euan's contract with club side Northampton, stating that he does not have to play club rugby on a Sunday, is thought to be unique in the sport.

OPENING UP

- What do you think about Euan's decision?

- How understanding do you think fans of his team are? What about when they narrowly lose in his absence?

- Why do you think Euan initially did play on a Sunday? What do you think changed his mind?

DIGGING DEEPER

- How often do you just do nothing (not even watch TV – just walk in the park or sit quietly)?

- How easy or difficult do you find it to switch off and relax completely? Why?

- How important is rest to you? Do you tend to rest too much or too little?

TAKING IT TO THE WORD

Read Exodus 20:8–11

- Why do you think God issues this commandment?

- Why does God say even servants and animals should rest?

- What does it mean for the seventh day to be "holy"? Is this the case in your life? How could you make it more holy?

SECTION C:
What would you do?

Introduction

At school, I always used to switch off during any discussion of "ethics", simply because it sounded like an incredibly dull and complicated subject. In fact, as I later discovered, ethics is actually an overarching concept which makes up an unavoidable element of all but the most uneventful days of our lives.

Put simply, ethics is the decisions we make about how we live. It's the way we navigate every life choice; the system by which we choose right from wrong. In the context of this collection of resources, it's a key part of every discussion. And contrary to my own teenage preconception, it's actually intensely interesting.

This section comprises a mix of true and fictional stories, each used to illustrate a question of ethics. Many of the stories are somewhat "ethically ambiguous"; designed to get young people to really talk and think about what they think – rather than telling them how. Although I have again supplied three banks of questions, here more than ever you will need to think on your feet as you lead the discussion, as your group will undoubtedly take things off in a far more interesting direction than I have envisaged here!

In my opinion – and don't be limited by it – these discussion starters will work really well in the context of an established group, or one in which you are trying to grow a sense of community. (Talk triggers like those collected in this book are great for getting young people to relate to one another properly for the first time.) If you are trying to take a group of teenagers on a journey of discipleship, questions of ethics – or how they apply their faith when the rubber hits the road – are a vital component.

So this section is all about outlining a tricky situation or morally ambiguous idea, and then asking young people: "what would you do?" Here, more than anywhere else, it's important to stress (and more importantly, demonstrate) that there are really no wrong answers – the important thing is to get young people thinking and talking.

C1

THEME: **Racism**

BIBLE: **Acts 17/Romans 10**

Black and white issue

An advertisement appears on the website of global software giants Microsoft. The main image depicts not only a fast-paced business environment, but an idealistic and modern one in which men and women, black and white, work together as equals. Unless, of course, you are viewing the Polish version.

Because, in a gaffe for which they soon apologized, Microsoft doctored the image on that version of the advert in order to remove the black face at the centre of the group, and replace it with the head of a white man. Compounding the mistake, they forgot to change the rest of the image, resulting in a composite central figure with a white face and black hands. The decision to do this – which Microsoft said it was investigating internally – created a PR disaster for the company, founded by billionaire businessman and philanthropist, Bill Gates.

The image was quickly circulated online by angry bloggers, who poked fun at the seemingly amateurish attempt to change the image, and expressed anger at a perceived act of racism. Like much of Eastern Europe, Poland has a different ethnic mix to the US and UK, and some bloggers have speculated that the image was changed in order to "reflect the demographics". Microsoft has since pulled the image from its websites.

OPENING UP

- Why do you think someone took the decision to doctor the photograph?

- The person responsible might argue that because there are fewer black people in Poland, they were simply adjusting the photo to better represent that country. What do you think of that argument?

- Is it ever right to discriminate on the basis of race or belief? Why or why not?

DIGGING DEEPER

- Have you or anyone you know ever been subjected to racist comments or worse? How did it feel for you/them?

- Why do you think people demonstrate racist beliefs?

- How do you think our society can continue to combat the rise of racism, and extremist groups who seek to discriminate on the basis of race?

TAKING IT TO THE WORD

Read Acts 17:26 and Romans 10:12

- How might the first verse be used to speak into this story?

- What does the second verse clearly teach about our attitude to people of other races?

- When do you find racial issues difficult? Pray together that God will use you as a force for good in a society that continues to wrestle with these issues.

C2

THEME: **Online friendship**

BIBLE: **1 Corinthians 13**

Morten gets hacked

Morten was a certified Facebook addict. Friends – his real ones that is, rather than the 1,000+ acquaintances he had "added" online – were forever commenting on how much time he spent on social networking websites. Every day, he would spend several hours posting photos, making and talking to virtual friends, taking irrelevant quizzes, and cataloguing every aspect of his real life online for all to see.

Unfortunately, security wasn't Morten's strong point. His Facebook password was a foolishly obvious choice, and when one of his many online "buddies" correctly guessed it, Morten was quickly plunged into no end of social trouble. The hacker wasted no time in ruining Morten's online life, deleting memorable photographs, posting rude comments on the pages of his closest friends, and setting his status to a string of swear words. Most maliciously of all, he even changed the account's password, so Morten was locked out – unaware of the level of carnage created.

Within minutes, Morten was receiving angry phone calls, texts, and emails from people telling him exactly what he could do with his "friendship". Unable to log back in and explain himself, he was devastated; his online dream had become a nightmare.

OPENING UP

- Do you feel sorry for Morten in this story, or is he partly to blame?

- What are some of the positives and negatives of his approach to social networking websites?

- Discuss your own online behaviour. What rules do you have about what you post online, how much you reveal about yourself, and who you connect with?

- Facebook "friendship" can be a cheap kind of friendship. What qualifies as a friend to you?

DIGGING DEEPER

- Why do you think social networking sites have become so popular?

- How honest do you think people are online? What might they be too honest about? What might they try to hide?

- How do you think social networking behaviour might change in the future?

TAKING IT TO THE WORD

Read 1 Corinthians 13:4–7

- This passage is often used at weddings, but it's really about the nature of God's love. How many of these qualities characterize your friendships?

- Can you demonstrate this kind of love on Facebook? If so, how?

- How might Morten be able to repair his damaged social life with the help of these verses?

C3

THEME: **Profit versus poverty**

BIBLE: **Isaiah 58/Jeremiah 5**

Where's our food?

Scorched by an unrelenting sun, almost 400,000 displaced people struggle for survival in a sprawling refugee camp in Northern Somalia. Faced with a daily battle to feed themselves and their children, they hope to somehow buck the statistics that have given their country one of the world's worst life expectancies. Forced from the capital Mogadishu by unending internal conflict, they live their lives in waiting: waiting for the fighting to end; waiting to see if today is the day when tragedy will strike.

Their lifeline is the World Food Programme; an internationally co-ordinated effort to ensure that enough food and sustenance finds its way to these impoverished desert communities. Governments and individuals have been generous; the world is not simply standing by and watching them starve. But there's a problem.

An undercover reporter, working for Britain's *Channel 4 News*, found compelling evidence that the food was not making its way into the desperate hands of its intended recipients. Instead, a seemingly huge percentage of these sacks, marked clearly with the WFP logo, were finding their way into the markets of Mogadishu. Salesmen blamed soldiers, escorts, and even corrupt WFP staff for the fact that food was being diverted into commercial hands. Whatever the explanation, this brutal capitalism is leaving dying children bereft of the food that the world had sent.

Meanwhile, the WFP country director for Somalia told the Channel 4 reporter of his unswerving belief that only a tiny percentage of food sacks were going missing. The accompanying TV pictures – of private warehouses full of WFP sacks – suggested otherwise.

OPENING UP

- How does this story make you feel?

- Why might the WFP country director claim that almost all the food was getting through?

- Where do you believe the blame lies for the tragedies in this story?

- We have provided aid, but it isn't getting through. What do you think the international community's response should be?

DIGGING DEEPER

- How do you think richer countries should help those which are suffering droughts and food shortages? Why those approaches?

- What are some of the reasons behind their poverty? Is there a way in which the West could be partly to blame?

TAKING IT TO THE WORD

Read Isaiah 58:6–11 and Jeremiah 5:26–29

- The first passage speaks about the role of God's followers.

What real action could this spur you to?

- The second passage talks about God's attitude to those who increase poverty, putting profit first. Why do you think these words, written so long ago, are so relevant today?

- How do these two passages impact the way you see poverty and need in your local community?

- Pray together, and agree ways, large and small, that you can begin to influence change and justice – where you are, and on a global scale.

C4

THEME: **Horror movies**

BIBLE: **Philippians 4**

Video nasty

Tom was a big-time horror movie buff. He obsessed over the latest instalments of every horror franchise, usually watching on DVD so that he could analyse the gruesome action over and again. Tom's favourite films involved dismemberment and torture – but almost always of people who had done something to "deserve it". There was another reason why Tom didn't catch these movies at the cinema though – they were all 18-certificates, and he was just 13.

Tom's DVD collection came courtesy of his dad, who didn't see a problem with his son watching these films as "they so obviously aren't real". So Tom became more and more immersed in this world of anger, violence, and desecration. In the evening, he would watch his latest favourite, and during school hours he would always have a notebook on the go, in which he would design his own instruments of death and torture. Deep down, he harboured hopes of becoming part of the horror movie industry when he was older.

Tom was quiet and had few friends, but one day one of them, Al, came over to his house for dinner. After they had eaten, Tom told Al about his movie collection.

Al had never seen an 18-certificate movie before, and was both scared and intrigued. Eventually, after much encouragement from Tom, he agreed to sit down and watch *Brainblender* – an ultra-hardcore horror film which Tom's dad had ordered from Korea.

Just a few minutes in, Al was feeling very sick and quite terrified. He hated the film, but didn't feel like he could admit that to Tom. After half an hour he could take no more: he made an excuse and left, leaving his friend disappointed. For the next week, Al suffered from terrible nightmares. Tom slept soundly.

OPENING UP

- Whose fault was it that this story ended badly? Al? Tom? Tom's dad? The film-makers?

- What might you have done in Al's position when Tom asked him to watch the movie?

- What do you think is the appeal of horror films?

- Do you agree with age ratings? Are they too high/low in your experience?

DIGGING DEEPER

- Why do you think Tom's sleep wasn't affected by the movie, while his friend suffered nightmares?

- How else may an addiction to horror films have been affecting Tom's life?

- What might watching hundreds of horror films do to Tom's own attitudes towards violence, suffering and real-life horror?

TAKING IT TO THE WORD

Read Philippians 4:4–9

- What do these verses suggest could be God's perspective on violent horror films?

- Do these verses make God sound boring, or suggest a better way? Explain your answer.

- What do you think might be the outcome of spending your time thinking about things that are "excellent, praiseworthy, admirable"? How might this affect you as a person?

C5

THEME: **Enemies**

BIBLE: **Luke 10**

Friendly rivalry?

Anthony and Rob were sworn rivals. Each played centre-forward for their under-18s football teams, both of which were located in the same town. Both of them desperately wanted to be the local hero, but since they were both brilliant players, there was little to choose between them.

So not only did both young men give 110 per cent on the pitch, they also obsessed about the other's performance. Anthony especially would scour local newspapers for match reports, focusing specifically on how Rob had done. Rob wasn't immune either: on his bedroom wall at home he kept a chart of the goals both of them had scored – and this season they were neck and neck.

Anthony often hoped that Rob would get an injury, which would allow him to storm ahead in the goal-scoring charts. Then, one night, he saw his wish unfold before his eyes. After a night out on the town, Anthony was walking home with friends when he heard the sound of a scuffle in a nearby alleyway. Investigating, he saw his great rival, Rob, in the middle of a fight with a gang of lads. Rob was already bleeding, but one of the gang was trying to wrestle him to the floor so that the attack could get nasty.

Anthony thought a terrible thought. If he and his friends simply walked on, Rob would probably receive bad enough injuries to stop him playing for a while. Anthony looked over at his friend Kobe, a six-and-a-half foot bodybuilder who was standing idle with a bag of chips. He knew that just the sight of Kobe would send the gang running for cover. What should he do?

Rob sounded like he was in real pain. As much as Anthony had made him a sworn enemy on the football pitch, he didn't deserve this. Anthony called to Kobe, who walked into the alley and broke up the fight with a couple of heavy punches. Rob emerged, cut and bruised, full of thanks to Anthony and his friends. He would never know how close they came to walking on by.

OPENING UP

- Can you empathize with what went through Anthony's mind?

- How would you have felt about him if he had walked on?

- Why do you think he chose not to?

DIGGING DEEPER

- Have you ever had an enemy or rival? Why did you find yourself pitched against them?

- Do you think there can be healthy rivalries? When do they become unhealthy?

- Have you ever seen someone as so much of an enemy that you wished them ill? Do you still feel that way? Why?

TAKING IT TO THE WORD

Read Luke 10:25–37

- This is a familiar story – why do you think Jesus tells it?

- A Samaritan would have been the man's deeply hated enemy. How do you think it felt to the man, to be saved by such a person?

- How do you think this story was heard and received by Jesus' crowd?

- How could you "go and do likewise" in your community?

C6

THEME:　**Toxic relationships**

BIBLE:　**Colossians 3**

Toxic Mark

Amelie was completely devoted to her boyfriend, Mark. He was the first boy who had ever shown any interest in her, and they had been together for nearly a year. In private, she would sit doodling, writing his name on a pad and drawing around it over and over again.

Mark wasn't the sort of boy her parents would approve of though. He was prominent in a large local group that wasn't quite a gang but sometimes behaved like one. He always seemed to be able to get hold of cannabis and occasionally other drugs, and sometimes he would get hold of it for others too.

What her parents would have really disapproved of, however, was the way he treated and spoke to their daughter. In private, he would be gentle and considerate – although that was partly because he seemed to be on a never-relenting quest to persuade her to sleep with him, even though she was underage. In public, however, he treated her like dirt.

When Amelie saw Mark in front of his friends, he wouldn't refer to her by name, but would use a string of derogatory words. Some of them she understood – she knew what a "bitch" and a "dog" were – but others were alien to her, and those were the ones that made the group laugh the most. In private, Mark would apologize, explaining that he just needed to keep his image up in the group.

At first, the words hurt Amelie; she would go home and cry, and even consider splitting up with Mark. But after a while they stopped having that effect. To please Mark, she would even laugh along when he called her those things. She allowed the words to become true for her. When alone, doodling in her bedroom, she began to write things like "Property of Mark" on her pad.

OPENING UP

- Why do you think Amelie continues to stay with Mark?

- Mark's words began to have less impact on her. Why? Is this a good or bad thing?

- Why do you think Mark was so different in private?

- What would your advice be if you met Amelie?

DIGGING DEEPER

- Does this story feel familiar? Do you feel girls are respected in your school or community?

- What influences do you think cause some boys to talk to girls like this?

- What does a healthy version of this relationship look like to you?

TAKING IT TO THE WORD

Read Colossians 3:1–17

- How do these verses outline how we should treat each other?

- How many of these things were reflected in your last relationship, or are in your current one?

- What kind of influence could this behaviour have on others? How might a boyfriend or girlfriend feel if they were treated like this? How might they even be changed themselves?

C7

THEME: **Gangs**

BIBLE: **Acts 4**

Initiation test

Simon felt like life had let him down. His dad had walked out before he was even born; stepfathers had come and gone; and his mum's interest in him seemed to decline with every passing year. Since his first year of school, he had always had a knack of falling into trouble, and teachers seemed to have his card marked even before he joined their classes.

At 14, Simon knew his life wasn't going anywhere. His grades were appalling; his financial situation was worse. He never had any money for anything, and he knew that his career prospects meant he probably never would. Life on his estate was okay, but sometimes it felt like the world kept on turning and he didn't move.

People thought Simon was a bad kid. He wasn't. He loved his grandma – the only person who ever showed interest in him, and doted on her. He even took her along to church sometimes to help her out.

Simon didn't mean to fall in with the wrong crowd. But the wrong crowd found him. One day, another boy of his age began to talk about a new "crew" in the area – a gang of lads who did everything together. The boy told him that the hand of friendship was being extended, and that Simon could choose to take it if he wanted.

It was a simple decision for Simon. After all, this group were offering him community, a sense of belonging – and apparently, no end of ways to make money. When he met the leaders, he saw that they were decked out in designer clothes and expensive jewellery. Some were even able to rent expensive apartments, even though they were just teenagers.

All Simon had to do was pass an initiation. And to his horror, he learned what that meant. He had to show commitment to the gang over anyone else – and that meant robbing his beloved grandma of her pension. The leader smirked as he watched Simon squirm. How could he do that? And yet, could he refuse?

OPENING UP

- This might seem like a clear-cut decision for Simon. Why might it not be?

- Would you have sympathy for Simon if he decided to steal from his grandma? Why or why not?

- Why do you think the gang asked him specifically to target her?

DIGGING DEEPER

- Are gangs always a negative thing? Why or why not?

- Why do you think gang membership is attractive to many young people? What does a gang offer that you can't get elsewhere?

- Why would someone choose membership of a gang over membership of a church or youth group? How are the two things similar and different?

TAKING IT TO THE WORD

Read Acts 4:32–37

- This was the first wave of church – does it sound like church as you know it? How is it similar or different?

- What would it look like if church was exactly like this today?

- Might it be more attractive even than gang membership? Why or why not?

- How could your group or expression of church look a little bit more like this?

C8

THEME: **Suffering**

BIBLE: **2 Corinthians 4**

Kellie's faith

Kellie had started the year full of optimism. She was due to sit her exams in the summer, and had been predicted great grades; she had just passed her driving test, and she had met the most amazing boy at church, and things really seemed to be going somewhere. She thought she might be falling in love. So on New Year's Eve, Kellie was brimming with excitement about the coming months.

Things didn't quite work out that way though. First, Kellie's dad suffered a massive stroke, and while he survived it, he was hugely debilitated by it. Then, Kellie caught her so-called "Mr Perfect" kissing one of her best friends at a birthday party. The relationship was finished at that moment, and Kellie began to wonder what kind of year this was going to be after all.

Then, just as she was preparing to take her final school exams, Kellie's car was hit by another driver, and she too had to spend time in hospital. Although she wasn't likely to suffer permanent side effects, both of her arms were broken; there was no way she would be able to sit the exams now – meaning she would also have to defer her university place.

So by the summer, this had proved to be the worst

year of Kellie's life. Yet, incredibly, she was able to find comfort in her faith. While many people might have been angry with God, or even begun to believe that the world was simply governed by ruthless fate, Kellie decided that God still had a plan for her life, and that he would teach her something through all this; that he was going to use all this pain for good somehow.

By the following New Year, things hadn't really improved. She still had trouble writing, she was still single, and her dad's recovery was slow. Yet, her friends were amazed that the one rock in her life was her constant belief in Jesus. While she had been shaken in so many ways, her faith had remained intact, and by the end of the year, many of her friends had seen their faith grow through her example.

OPENING UP

- Are you surprised that Kellie retained such a strong faith in God? Why?

- How do you think God had perhaps already started to use Kellie's situation for good?

- What do you think went through Kellie's head as her suffering began to pile up?

DIGGING DEEPER

- How does suffering affect your faith if you have one?

- How else do you react to it? Does it get on top of you, or encourage you to respond in a different way?

- Have you ever seen excitement and hope dashed? What did it feel like? How did you respond?

TAKING IT TO THE WORD

Read 2 Corinthians 4:7–18

- What does it mean to have "treasure in jars of clay"? What's the writer getting at?

- How does this passage help us to make sense of pain, weakness and failure?

- Do you find this passage encouraging, scary, or something else?

C9

THEME: **Peacemaking**

BIBLE: **James 3**

Class war

Class 9ED had once been such a close-knit group of girls. Thrown together more than two years ago (as 7AJ), they had managed to laugh and learn together in fairly equal amounts. No one had felt left out, there wasn't any bullying or strong rivalry; even their teachers looked forward to taking the class.

Until one thing happened. Or even, maybe, didn't happen.

It started when Cara told Sophie about something she had overheard, and then Sophie told the Lister twins, and one of them wrote something on the board, and suddenly it had turned into a full-blown rumour. No one was really that sure if it was even true. Cara insisted it was: some girls in the top maths set had made a joke about the girls in the bottom one.

The class divided in half, along lines of mathematical ability. The bottom set girls felt alienated, upset and betrayed; those in the top set couldn't understand what all the fuss was about. Friendships splintered, the atmosphere evaporated, and the teachers were suddenly looking for every excuse not to teach 9ED. Even Mr Daniels, their form tutor, developed an uncanny knack of missing morning registration because his "car was so unreliable".

Anna seemed to be the one member of 9ED who was immune to the split. She still managed to have friends on both sides of the divide – although they weren't particularly happy that she wouldn't pick a side.

Anna knew she had to do something about the split in her class. It was making life uncomfortable for teachers, pupils, and parents alike. Nobody could even remember what the argument was about in the first place – but what could she do?

OPENING UP

- What *could* Anna do? Do you think there's anything practical that she could do to end the feud?

- How would you have felt if you had been in the bottom maths set and learned that the people in the other set looked down on you?

- Why do you think this seemingly perfect class community disintegrated so quickly?

DIGGING DEEPER

- What does it mean to be a "peacemaker"?

- How can people make peace in different situations – in churches, families, communities, etc.?

- What is peace? Is it important? Is it always the best option?

TAKING IT TO THE WORD

Read James 3:13–18

- What are the two kinds of "wisdom" outlined here?

- What does verse 18 mean?

- How can you be a peacemaker in your school, family or elsewhere?

C10

THEME: **White lies?**

BIBLE: **Luke 16**

"Mis-Judged"

It started out with a "little white lie", and it ended with a three-year jail term. And this isn't the story of a foolish young man, but the remarkable fall from grace of one of Australia's most respected judges.

Marcus Einfield had been at the top of his profession for many years by the time he was awarded the status of "National Living Treasure" by the National Trust of Australia. Today, he is no longer acknowledged as such, and again, it's because of a single lie.

What happened? In 2006, Einfield was caught by a speed camera in Sydney travelling just six miles over the limit. The offence would cost the multi-millionaire around £35, and add two penalty points to his driving licence. At the age of 68, it was hardly going to blight his glittering career.

Yet, inexplicably, Einfield chose to lie. He told a magistrate that he hadn't been driving the car at the time, and had in fact lent it to a friend, American professor Theresa Brennan. Satisfied with this explanation from such a pillar of the national community, the magistrate allowed Einfield to get off without paying the fine.

Brennan's was an odd name for the judge to have chosen, particularly because she had died in America three years earlier. When a local newspaper did a little research and uncovered that fact, Einfield was back in the legal spotlight. At this point, had he come clean about his "white lie", he might still have walked away with his reputation virtually intact. Yet, he didn't – he decided to dig deeper, and tell another untruth.

No, it wasn't *that* Theresa Brennan, he claimed. Committed now, he went away and created a fictionalized 20-page account of another woman by that name, and his dealings with her. The police were unconvinced, and the judge began to squirm as officers searched his home and computer. Eventually the web of lies collapsed, and the judge was charged with making a false statement under oath and attempting to pervert the course of justice. He was sentenced to three years in jail – leaving his reputation in tatters – all for a £35 fine and two penalty points.

OPENING UP

- Why do you think the judge lied in the first place?

- How do you think he felt when his first lie was uncovered by journalists? Why do you think he chose to lie again?

- At what point do you think he regretted his lie?

- Do you think he ever believed his lie would land him in this degree of trouble? Why do you think it did?

DIGGING DEEPER

- What is a "white lie"? Why do you think it's called that, and why do you think it's seen as being socially acceptable?

- Is it ever OK to lie? If so, when?

- How would you feel if someone lied to you "to protect you", and then you found out?

- Have you ever seen a lie backfire? What happened?

TAKING IT TO THE WORD

Read Luke 16:10–12 (you may wish to read 1–9 as context)

- Is Jesus right? Why or why not? How might you argue against him?

- What is the difference between "worldly wealth" and "true riches"?

- Look also at these Proverbs: 12:19; 12:22; 13:5; 19:5. What are some of the messages here about lying?

C11

THEME: **Torture/justification**

BIBLE: **Romans 3**

The end justifies the means?

Secret agent Jack Bauer is a man with no need for sleep, love, or it would seem, toilet breaks. As the focal point of the action in hit TV show *24*, he's never far from danger, international incident, and potential catastrophe.

Jack is someone who lives by the mantra "the end justifies the means". Regularly in the show, our "hero" finds himself tracking a trail toward some criminal mastermind or other; usually a man who is hell-bent on carnage and destruction. Sometimes, a vial of a terrible killer gas has been hidden somewhere; other times there's a nuclear threat hanging over Los Angeles. One thing's always for sure though – if Jack doesn't get to the bottom of things, people will die.

As Jack follows his trail, he inevitably finds himself faced with people who refuse to talk. Where others who play by the rules might then be scratching their heads, however, Jack simply unpacks his portable torture kit, and begins inflicting unimaginable agony on these lower-rung terrorists, until they eventually break down and tell him where the bigger fish are hiding.

Of course, *24* is a television show, and Jack Bauer isn't real. But are scenes like this completely imagined, or based on possible fact? Amnesty International – the human rights charity – reports that in the period between 1997 and 2000, at least 150 countries were guilty of state-sponsored torture. In many of those cases, that torture was used to allow officials to force information out of prisoners – and in some cases that information will almost certainly have saved lives. So is Jack Bauer right? Does the end justify the means?

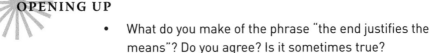

OPENING UP

- What do you make of the phrase "the end justifies the means"? Do you agree? Is it sometimes true?

- What is the alternative to torture for someone like Jack Bauer?

- Is it better that innocent people die, but human rights are preserved? Or vice versa?

- In a show like *24*, or a film featuring Bourne or Bond, how aware are you of the ethics of the way the "hero" behaves? Do you think about it?

DIGGING DEEPER

- Do you believe torture is as widespread as Amnesty International claims?

- What are some of the reasons that a person, state or agency might choose to torture someone?

- What do you think the international community's response to Amnesty's claim should be?

TAKING IT TO THE WORD

Read Romans 3:5–8

- Paul reveals that people had claimed that the early Christians "did evil that good may result". Why might people have made that claim?

- What is Paul's response to the question "Does the end justify the means?" (verse 8)?

C12

THEME: **Celibacy**

BIBLE: **Romans 3**

Jill's decision, Clare's mistake

As one of the most conventionally beautiful people in her church youth group, Jill was never short of male attention. Yet, while she had had a couple of kisses with boys at parties, and one very brief "relationship" with a boy who was too scared of her beauty to even hold her hand, Jill had got to 16 without very much involvement with boys at all.

At school, some of the girls who were jealous of her tried to circulate a rumour that she was gay, but there was no foundation to it and it soon drifted away. Some of the more confident lads started to see her as a trophy, and would invest more and more time and effort into trying to romance her.

None of it worked. A Christian from a young age, Jill had made a decision in her early teens to save sex for when she was married. Working backwards, she had then decided that she didn't want to fall into the trap of doing "everything but". Sex in its broadest sense was something she wanted to keep as a gift for her future husband. At first this was a private decision, but after a while she decided to go public, talking about it openly at her youth group, and becoming a role model for many of the younger girls for that reason.

There was one girl, however, who didn't look up to Jill. Every time Clare heard her talking about celibacy and purity, it made her feel angry and ashamed. Until they were both 15, Clare had followed the same promise, but one night at a party that all changed. It was with a boy she didn't know, it lasted barely ten minutes, and it hurt. Immediately, she regretted what she had done, and had prayed to God for forgiveness. The boy, meanwhile, had gone straight downstairs to tell everyone what had happened.

Everyone at school and at church knew about Clare's mistake. Her youth leaders told her how disappointed they were; her friends gave her a cruel nickname. Now, every time she heard Jill talking about the joys of waiting for sex, she just felt lonely and ashamed.

OPENING UP

- Do you sympathize with Clare? Why or why not?

- Why do you think she feels "lonely and ashamed"?

- What advice might you give to her now?

- How do you think Jill has managed to remain a virgin at 16?

- What could Jill do to make sure her positive message doesn't become a painful one for people like Clare?

DIGGING DEEPER

- How much pressure is there on young people to be sexually active?

- Do you think it's realistic to ask people to wait until they are married to have sex? Why?

- What might be some of the benefits of waiting? And the drawbacks?

- Why do you think so many people regret their first sexual experience?

TAKING IT TO THE WORD

Read 1 Corinthians 7:2, then Romans 3:21–26

- What does the first verse suggest about God's view of sex outside of marriage?

- Why do you think that is his view?

- How does the passage from Romans reassure us if we have made mistakes?

- Does that mean we can just sin now and apologize later? (Romans 6:1–2 may help.)

C13

THEME: **Capital punishment**

BIBLE: **John 8**

Just punishment?

At the time of writing, Troy Davis has spent nineteen on death row in a United States jail – sentenced to death for a crime that he has always claimed he did not commit.

In 1989, off-duty police officer Mark MacPhail was murdered in Savannah, Georgia. He had been working a second job as a security guard at a Burger King restaurant when he responded to the shouts of a homeless man. Troy Davis was talking to friends nearby, and claims to have only watched what unfolded, as someone fired a .38-calibre gun at MacPhail. The officer died at the scene, a dark and chaotic car park. Another man, Redd Coles, who was of similar height, weight and build to Troy, was also at the scene. Both men were African Americans.

Even though a spent shell from a gun belonging to Coles was found at the scene, and there was only witness-based evidence against Troy, it was the latter who found himself charged with the officer's murder. In 1991, he was sentenced to death for the crime, which he repeatedly insisted he was not responsible for.

Over the next nineteen years, Troy went through a series of appeals, many of which seemed to split juries on the case. The police maintained his guilt; a number of human rights organizations, including Amnesty International, continued to campaign for his release. According to Amnesty, seven of the original nine witnesses have now changed or withdrawn their testimonies, with several claiming they were coerced by police into saying certain things.

Troy continues to face the prospect of being executed for murder – a punishment which some would argue does not fit any crime. Yet, it's very possible that he could be killed as an innocent man – delivering a very warped kind of justice for the family of Mark MacPhail.

OPENING UP

- Why do you think their remains such doubt about this case, more than twenty years after the death of Mark MacPhail?

- Do you think Mark's family would feel a sense of justice or closure if Troy was executed?

- Why do you think it appears the police were so keen to see Troy convicted?

DIGGING DEEPER

- What are some of the good reasons against the death penalty?

- What might be some arguments in its favour?

- Which side of the line do you sit? Are there some crimes for which you think it's appropriate? Why?

TAKING IT TO THE WORD

Read John 8:1–11

- Here, Jesus interrupts an Old Testament-sanctioned execution (Exodus 21–24). How can he do this?

- How does Jesus' coming remove the need for a death penalty? What does he open the way for?

- Why is Jesus' command for the woman to "leave her life of sin" important in understanding his view of the death penalty?

C14

THEME: **Revenge**

BIBLE: **Romans 12**

Appetite for destruction

It started with a terrible mistake, but it just kept growing and growing. All-out war had broken out between two gangs who lived on neighbouring housing estates in London.

A year earlier, the two tribes had barely bothered each other. Yet, when the girlfriend of the first gang's leader slept with a local boy, and he was wrongly identified as Tony, a member of the other gang, all hell broke loose. Two senior gang members hunted down Tony – who was innocent – and stabbed him in the street, leaving him for dead.

Tony survived, just, but knew the names of the young men who had attacked him. Instead of going to the police, he demanded revenge, and with the agreement of his leader, the gang went after them. This time, the attack resulted in a death. While the police were involved, no one gave them any names. This was to be sorted out internally.

And so it went on – two gangs, repeatedly going after each other in the name of revenge – with a perverted sense of justice. By the end of the year, lives had been lost on both sides; several more people had been stabbed. One of them was an innocent bystander, a young woman caught in the wrong place at the wrong time. It didn't stop the bloodshed. The battle for revenge went on and on.

OPENING UP

- How do you think this story will end?

- Do you think this story is realistic? If so, what are some of the factors in society that make such a horrible story possible?

- What might be some ways that this cycle of violence could be stopped? How could the gang members find a solution? What outside agencies could get involved?

DIGGING DEEPER

- Have you ever wanted to take revenge on someone? Why? What happened?

- How does it feel (or how do you think it feels) to take out revenge on someone who has wronged you?

- Do you think it's sometimes "just" to take revenge on people? If so, in what circumstances?

TAKING IT TO THE WORD

Read Romans 12:14–21

- What are some of the many things Paul says here that could speak into this situation?

- How is vengeance the Lord's? Do you think he strikes people down with bolts of lightning?

- How easy or difficult is the approach Paul is suggesting? How could we possibly live like this?

- How would your community change if these ideas were implemented there?

C15

THEME: **Slimming**

BIBLE: **1 Samuel 16**

Fat boy slims

Joe had always been a chunky child. Partly, it was because his mum insisted on serving chips with everything from the moment he was on to solid food, and partly it was because he was just born that way.

One summer in his early teens, Joe suddenly discovered girls. As a member of an all-boys school, he had had little cause to meet many of them before; but when he did, he liked them. They were pretty, they made him feel funny inside, and they smelled good enough to... well, eat. While his friends all soon picked up girlfriends, however, Joe was left holding the hamburger of loneliness. And one day, when he finally plucked up the courage to ask out one of the girls – and received a crushing rejection – Joe decided that enough was enough.

For the rest of the summer, Joe disappeared. When school reconvened, his friends were shocked by what they saw. Joe's body had slimmed dramatically, and while he was still a little plump, he was certainly no longer deserving of most of his nicknames. Joe revealed that he had been hard at work in the gym, and that he had committed himself to a strict diet (which meant not eating any of his mum's cooking).

At first, Joe's friends were very impressed. A couple of the girls in his peer group even began to show an interest in him. But after a while, people began to worry. Joe was still losing weight at a dramatic rate, and no one had seen him eat anything for months. Instead of just looking slim, Joe began to look gaunt and ghostly. When anyone challenged him, he claimed to eat huge breakfasts at home – which was a lie – and told them that he was still pretty flabby.

He wasn't. In six months, Joe had almost completely disappeared. Still, he maintained his hectic gym schedule. He didn't get a girlfriend though; a couple of the girls even commented that they liked him better when he was chubby.

OPENING UP

- What do you think has happened to Joe in this story? What advice would you give him?

- Why do you think Joe connected being slim with winning over the opposite sex? Why didn't this happen in reality?

- Do you think Joe is happy at the end of the story?

DIGGING DEEPER

- Do you think boys or girls are more obsessed with their body image?

- Where do we get our ideas about what a "good" body is? Is this healthy?

- What can we do to counteract some of the media messages about what a "normal" body is?

TAKING IT TO THE WORD

Read 1 Samuel 16:1–7

- What is happening in this story?

- How does the way God views us differ from the way we see each other? How does this make you feel? Scared? Comforted?

- How can we be more like God in looking at each other's "hearts" more?

- What might you say to Joe as a response to these verses?

C16

THEME: **Euthanasia**

BIBLE: **Proverbs 24**

Right to die?

Gail was in her late 30s when she first noticed that something wasn't right. By her early 40s, she was in the full grip of a terrible, debilitating syndrome called Motor Neurone Disease. Little by little, her illness was robbing her of her independence, and despite advances in medicine, she was often in great pain. Her speech became more and more slurred, and she became unable to look after herself.

Gail was horrified by what had happened to her. There was no cure for her condition, and the prognosis was that she would continue to deteriorate, but live for many more years. This wasn't something Gail felt she wanted.

By talking to other sufferers, Gail learned about the Dignitas group in Switzerland – an organization who help sufferers of incurable diseases to take their own lives. Quickly, she made up her mind that she wanted to travel to Switzerland and take her death into her own hands.

There was a problem though. To get to Dignitas, Gail would need help, and her daughter, Faye, was the most likely person to give it. When she shared her idea,

Faye was devastated and immediately refused. As she watched her mum suffer even more painful deterioration though, she began to wonder: what was the right thing to do?

OPENING UP

- What would the "right" thing be for Faye to do here?

- How do you think Gail felt as she watched herself deteriorate?

DIGGING DEEPER

- Do we have a "human right" to die?

- How do you think you might feel if you knew you were destined to deteriorate into a painful and incurable condition? Would you consider assisted dying (euthanasia)?

- Why do you think some people – not necessarily those with a religious conviction – think euthanasia is wrong?

TAKING IT TO THE WORD

Read Proverbs 24:8–12

- What does it mean to "rescue those being led away to death"?

- What do these verses seem to suggest about killing?

- Exodus 20:13 says "you shall not murder". What is murder? Is euthanasia somehow different?

C17

THEME: **Masculinity**

BIBLE: **Ruth 3**

Boys behaving badly

Taye and Ben were, to be painfully honest, the only good-looking young men in their youth group. They went to a female-dominated youth group in a church that was also about 70 per cent female, and for some reason, they found that neither of them was able to settle with just one woman.

At age 17, they had both been in the group for three years, and there was a problem. Between them, they had dated every girl in the group, and in many cases, they had both dated the same girl. They had countless physical experiences with the girls in the group – although they both swore they were still virgins and claimed to take their Christian faith very seriously. When a new young woman arrived at church or at the group, both of them would instantly appear beside her, like a pair of baying, competing wolves. Several girls never came back for that very reason.

Taye and Ben's youth worker, Colin, was a much older man, married with four children. He suggested that perhaps they needed to become more responsible in their attitudes to the opposite sex. To Colin's face, both boys agreed.

Privately though, they laughed together about their meeting with Colin. Neither of them were looking for a serious relationship, and they couldn't see the harm in having "a little fun". That Sunday, when a new girl arrived at youth group, the wolves were still on the prowl, just a little more stealthily.

OPENING UP

- Do you recognize the characters of Taye and Ben? Or at least some of their characteristics?

- Why do you think some Christian men behave in this way?

- Why would Taye and Ben have found it hard to take Colin seriously?

DIGGING DEEPER

- Why are there generally more women than men in church congregations?

- Do you think church is geared more towards men or women?

- Where do Christian men get their ideas of masculinity from? How could this be improved?

TAKING IT TO THE WORD

Read Ruth 3:7–14 (you may wish to explain the concept of a kinsman-redeemer)

- How is Boaz's response to Ruth inspiring?

- How does this inform how a Christian man should act?

- How does Boaz protect Ruth's integrity, and his own?

- What are some of the characteristics of a good Christian man?

C18

THEME: **Charity**

BIBLE: **2 Corinthians 9**

Charity stays at home

Klaus was a very fortunate young man, and he knew it. He came from a very wealthy family, in a long line of very wealthy families. He had every new gadget almost before it was in the shops; owned a sports car even though he was still not quite old enough to drive it; had a Blu-Ray DVD collection that was big enough for him to open his own rental shop. He was also used to living in supreme comfort, and was the only 16-year-old he knew to have an en-suite bathroom AND personal living room.

Klaus was also generous with his money, and that ensured he was always very popular. He was one of the central figures in his church youth group, and not just because of his wealth. He was also funny, kind, and a good listener.

When the youth leader announced that he was organizing a trip abroad for the group, everyone hoped that Klaus would put his name down. At first, Klaus thought he would do so too. But when the leader announced that the trip was to Romania, and that the group would be living in very basic accommodation in order to help build a new hospital and orphanage, Klaus quickly changed his mind. He simply couldn't imagine spending ten days in squalor.

Klaus knew his decision had upset the group, so he set about trying to "fix" it. He asked his father if he could make a sizeable donation to the building fund for the orphanage, and his father agreed. Klaus thought his announcement that he was donating £10,000 would thrill everyone and make them happy with him again.

It didn't though. Instead, his friends challenged him that he should still come along on the trip, because, maybe, it would be good for him as well as the group. Klaus could not believe how ungrateful the group, and even his youth leader, were. Now he was even more sure he wasn't going to go on the trip.

OPENING UP

- Do you sympathize with Klaus? Is it fair that his generosity was received so poorly?

- Why do you think the group were disappointed that Klaus wasn't going to join them?

- What would you say to Klaus?

- How will Klaus miss out by only giving financially? How will others miss out?

DIGGING DEEPER

- Do you, or would you like to, give to charity? Why?

- What are some of the arguments against charitable giving?

- Is giving financially the best way to donate to charity? What other ways are there?

- What would be a balanced approach to charitable giving?

TAKING IT TO THE WORD

Read 2 Corinthians 9:6–15

- What approach to giving is encouraged here?

- What does it mean to be a "cheerful giver"?

- Paul mentions "good work" and "service" as he talks about generosity – what does this suggest about a balanced approach to giving?

Betty done 17/2/13.

C19

THEME: **Cheating**

BIBLE: **Galatians 6**

Exam scam

It sounded too good to be true. For just £100, Chris was being offered the exact maths exam paper that he was about to sit in a week. A man who said he worked for the exam board had approached Chris and his friends with the offer – £100 cash for the paper.

Chris couldn't believe his luck. He had been leaving his revision to the last minute anyway, and he knew he was unlikely to get the grades he needed to get into university. Here, for a relatively small sum of money, he had the opportunity to cheat his way to an "A" grade. Without even thinking, he raided his bank account for the money and handed it over.

For a moment, Chris suddenly wondered if he had been scammed. He didn't know this man – he might have been a total fraud. But sure enough, he came back with the paper, and it certainly looked real enough. Chris took the paper and devoured it, working out all the correct answers using text books and the Internet. Then he memorized his answers, as well as some realistic methods of "working out".

On the day of the exam, Chris knew that if this was really a fake, then he was completely sunk. But it wasn't a fake. As Chris opened the paper his heart leapt – the answers in his head could get him a 100 per cent score if he wanted one. Of course, that would be unrealistic, so he thought he would aim for about 80 per cent – still easily enough for an "A".

As Chris was scribbling the answers down, however, he was overcome by a feeling of guilt. He was going to ace the exam, and yet, he hadn't earned it at all. Feeling like he had no other option, Chris fully completed the test as planned. When the inevitable "A" grade arrived his family were amazed and showered him with gifts. Chris knew the truth though, and he felt empty.

OPENING UP

- How do you feel about Chris at the end of this story?

- What do you think you might have done if you were in his position, and offered a copy of the exam paper in advance? Why?

- Did Chris have another option when he felt guilty, other than to complete the exam as planned?

DIGGING DEEPER

- Why is cheating in tests wrong? Who does it hurt?

- Is cheating ever right or justifiable? When?

- Have you ever cheated? How did it feel? What happened?

TAKING IT TO THE WORD

Read Galatians 6:7–8

- These are quite harsh words. What do you think they mean?

- What view do you think God takes of cheating? Do you think sometimes there are incidences where he doesn't mind so much? Why?

- What would your advice to Chris be in the light of these verses?

C20

THEME: **Homosexuality**

BIBLE: **James 2/Romans 1**

Feeling different

Rhiannon had gone through a wild-child period in her early teens when she had made an awful lot of mistakes. She had rebelled against her parents, who were church leaders, and had messed around with boys, drugs and alcohol. At 15, she then shocked everyone by becoming a Christian at a big youth camp, which she had only attended in the first place because it gave her a chance to escape.

So at 15, everything changed. She calmed down, started going to church and Christian Union, and even got herself a suitably wet and woolly boyfriend, Chris. He liked to lead Bible studies and go for long walks, but romantically speaking, wasn't interested in anything more than a peck on the cheek. Rhiannon liked the relationship though – it made her feel safe, and seemed to demonstrate to her that life had changed.

Rhiannon's youth leaders put her in a prayer partnership with Laura, a pretty girl from a different school who Rhiannon had never met before. They got on like a house on fire, and started to meet up more and more regularly. At first, they would just meet before school to pray, but soon they were having movie nights in, going to parties together, and generally hanging out all the time. Chris, who was too feeble to argue anyway, was often disappointed to find out that his girlfriend was too busy to see him, because as usual, she was with Laura.

Over time, however, Rhiannon began to realize that she felt something more for Laura – something she had never felt for Chris. When her times with Laura came to an end, she would begin to feel heartbroken – as if she was in love. At first she was horrified, and couldn't understand why she was feeling this way. Soon though, she began to think that this might mean something else. Was she gay?

OPENING UP

- Do you think Rhiannon is definitely gay? What would your advice be to her?

- What could be another way of interpreting Rhiannon's story?

- What would the reaction be in your group if Rhiannon was a member and chose to "come out" as a lesbian? Do you think that would be the right reaction?

DIGGING DEEPER

- How would you react if one of your best friends told you they were gay?

- What's your view on homosexuality? Accepting? Condemning? Something else?

- Why do you think there is still great prejudice in society against homosexual people?

- Should Bible-believing Christians stand against them?

TAKING IT TO THE WORD

Read James 2:1–4

- How does God feel about prejudice?

- Do you think these verses just apply to wealth and class? Could they also apply to homophobia?

Read Romans 1:24–27

- What does Paul appear to say about homosexuality here?

- What should be our approach to homosexual people in the light of both these sets of verses?

C21

THEME: **War**

BIBLE: **1 Chronicles 22**

A just war?

On 20 March 2003, the United States invaded Iraq, backed by the United Kingdom and a small group of other countries. Their objective was to overthrow the regime of the despotic Saddam Hussein.

One of the main motivations for invasion, for both British and American politicians, was the claim that Hussein was harbouring Weapons of Mass Destruction (WMDs), which they believed contained chemical and possibly even nuclear warheads. British intelligence claimed that the weapons could be readied by the Iraqis within 45 minutes of Hussein giving the order.

In April, the major Iraqi strongholds were captured, and Hussein went into hiding (he was later discovered hiding underground). By 1 May, the end of "major combat operations" was declared, as the *invasion* became an *occupation*.

Fighting between US and British forces and Iraqi insurgents continued for many years, however, and at time of writing, is still going on. According to one claim, over 1.3 million people have so far lost their lives as a result of the Iraq War.

Before the invasion had even taken place, however,

the British people had been very clear of their lack of support for the war. A demonstration in London, one of 800 similar demonstrations in cities worldwide, attracted 1–2 million people. Worldwide, 6–10 million people protested, but the London protest was particularly significant because of Britain's role in the proposed invasion. Needless to say, despite the unprecedented show of public opposition, then Prime Minister Tony Blair took his country to war anyway. Incidentally, evidence for Iraq's supposed Weapons of Mass Destruction was never found.

OPENING UP

- Do you think George Bush and Tony Blair would have made the same decision today if they had known in advance what the consequences would be?

- How do you think Tony Blair justified his decision to ignore the protests?

- How does this make you view the idea of protesting?

- How does the Iraq War affect your views on war?

DIGGING DEEPER

- Is war ever justified? When?

- What should be the aims of a "good" force in a war?

- Do you think peace campaigners are being naïve?

TAKING IT TO THE WORD

Read 1 Chronicles 22:5–10

- What is the general perception around the Old Testament God's view of war?

- What does God's word to David reveal about his true view of war?

- Why does God only want a man of peace to build his temple?

- Do these verses surprise you in any way?

C22

THEME: **Laziness/divorce**

BIBLE: **Proverbs 26**

Lazy boy

Aaron had never really recovered from his parents' messy divorce. His dad had become distant and moved in with another woman; his mum had become angry and bitter. Aaron had taken to living in his room, which had its own sofa, DVD player, and games console. He didn't want to talk to friends about what had happened, and he certainly didn't want to see his family.

Aaron's sister Jo, who had suffered just as much, was coping better though. However, a year on from their parents' split, she was beginning to worry about Aaron. Apart from going to school – which he often missed – her brother barely ever left the house. Or even his room.

Eventually Jo confronted Aaron about his behaviour, and asked him when he was going to start living again. His reply was "never". In his mind at least, there weren't good enough reasons to restart the sort of social life he used to enjoy.

He made one other promise to Jo – that he would definitely never get married. Right now, even the idea of a relationship felt horrible to him.

OPENING UP

- Why do you think Aaron had turned against the idea of relationships? Do you think this is a common feeling when people's parents divorce?

- Do you sympathize with Aaron? What would your advice to him be?

- Why do you think Aaron and Jo reacted so differently?

DIGGING DEEPER

- Is it good to have lots of technology and comforts in your bedroom? Why or why not?

- Do you understand why Aaron became so lazy? Have you ever had a period like that?

- Why does divorce have such a shattering impact on children?

TAKING IT TO THE WORD

Read Proverbs 26:13–16

- Do these verses seem harsh? Why or why not?

- How is Aaron doing what's described in verse 13?

- What are some of the consequences of the kind of laziness attributed to "the sluggard" here?

- Why do you think the Bible is so strong on the sin of laziness?

- In what ways are you a "sluggard"? How could you improve in these areas?

C23

THEME: **Abortion**

BIBLE: **Psalm 139**

Keeping Amy

When Felicity got pregnant, everyone seemed to have an opinion. Her dad told her she was an irresponsible idiot; her mum told her that, at 15, she was in danger of ruining her life. The baby was a result of a one-night-stand at a party, and her very first sexual experience.

Even though she came from a Christian family, both of Felicity's parents believed that an abortion was "the only sane answer". Her dad booked her in for a termination himself, the day after finding out about the pregnancy.

The few friends in whom Felicity confided all agreed with her parents – if she kept the baby, she would struggle to enjoy the next ten years of her life. No boys would want to be with her, and she could say goodbye to peaceful sleep. Her best friend, Jen, thought she should have the baby and offer it up for adoption. Others tried to dissuade her from this though – if only because of horrible stretch marks she could be left with.

The day of the planned termination arrived, and Felicity's dad drove his daughter and Jen to the clinic. When she arrived though, she thought that she felt the baby kick inside her. Her dad told her that she was imagining things, but Jen said she thought it was a "sign". Felicity agreed, and, incurring her dad's fury, cancelled the termination.

Several months later, baby Amy was born. Felicity's parents, who had had time to think, helped her to identify a loving family who would adopt her.

OPENING UP

- What do you think Jen meant when she said the kick had been "a sign"? Do you believe this sort of thing really happens?

- Why do you think so many people around Jen thought she should have an abortion?

- How do you feel about her parents' reactions?

DIGGING DEEPER

- What is society's general view on abortion today? What is your view?

- When do you think life begins?

- Why do you think that when women miscarry, people say they have lost "a baby", but when women have an abortion, they don't use that word?

TAKING IT TO THE WORD

Read Psalm 139:13–16

- What does this passage suggest is the missing element from the scientific view of reproduction?

- Can it be right for man to destroy a foetus if it is truly made in this way? Why or why not?

- How do these verses make you feel about yourself?

C24

THEME: **Respecting authority**

BIBLE: **Romans 13**

The parish letter

Michael was the new curate at St John's Parish Church, a large parish church in the centre of a big town. He had just left training college, and was full of big ideas about how the church can transform community. He wanted to see youth and children's groups explode into life; dreamed of running a night shelter for local homeless people, and had even written his own evangelistic course, which was in his words at least, "miles better than Alpha".

When Michael arrived, however, he found his way was blocked. The church's elderly vicar, Samuel, liked to "keep things consistent". He was worried by the idea of big change, and believed that the way they were doing things already was working well.

Michael was furious with Samuel's response to his ideas. How could this old man possibly still be in touch with what people needed? Why did he want to keep church the same when so many thousands of local people simply never came near it?

While he was still angry, Michael wrote a long open letter to the church's members. Even though he had only been at St John's for a matter of weeks, he could already see all the faults with the church, and with Samuel's leadership of it. In his letter, he explained all the problems in great detail, and outlined each of his brilliant solutions to them.

A week later, Michael was asked to leave the church. It wasn't Samuel's decision – in fact, he had urged people to show understanding to the younger man. But Michael's letter had stirred up so much anger among the congregation (who, as it turned out, thought Samuel was doing a pretty great job), it was simply impossible for the curate to stay.

OPENING UP

- Do you sympathize with Michael? Why or why not?

- What do you think Michael will learn from this?

- Why was Michael perhaps unwise to write his letter while he was still angry? How might he have behaved differently if he had calmed down first?

DIGGING DEEPER

- How easy do you find it to be led by others? At school? At church? Elsewhere?

- In what cases is it sometimes difficult to submit to people in authority over us?

- Is it ever right to stand up to authority instead of submitting? How do we judge when that time is?

TAKING IT TO THE WORD

Read Romans 13:1–7

- How is a rebellion against authority also a rebellion against God?

- What does this mean if we want to challenge authority?

- What are the reasons for submitting to authority?

- How right or easy do these verses sound to implement in your own life?

- Where do you need to respect authority more?

C25

THEME: **Cyber-bullying**

BIBLE: **Matthew 5**

Not fine online

At school, Paul was popular enough. He had a good group of friends, enjoyed playing sport, and – while he spent a little too much time in the computer room – had developed a normal personality. Offline then, Paul's world was a happy one.

Online, however, Paul had a problem. Online, Paul had enemies.

Whenever Paul logged in to one of his social network pages, he would wince. Had someone hacked into his account again, and posted disgusting messages supposedly from him? Would he have another inbox full of messages poking fun at his looks and his inability to get a girlfriend?

Paul loved going online because as a computer and gaming nut, that was where half his world lay. Yet, every time he did so, he knew that the two or three cyber-bullies, at least one of whom he knew in real life, were likely to come after him again. He didn't understand what could possibly motivate them to hound him like this.

If Paul had been bullied in the playground, he might have gone to a teacher or youth worker for support. Because his bullying was all taking place online, however, Paul felt strangely embarrassed by the idea of telling anyone. Surely they would just tell him to pull himself together? It was only virtual anyway.

It didn't feel virtual though. Although his bullies hid behind avatars, their arrows hit their target. Paul's feelings of hurt and despair were very real.

OPENING UP

- Do you understand why Paul doesn't feel able to talk to a teacher or youth worker?

- What advice would you give Paul?

- What do you think is motivating the bullies to keep pestering him?

DIGGING DEEPER

- Have you experienced cyber-bullying? How does it differ to "offline" bullying?

- Why do you think people behave as bullies online when they would never do so in real life?

- How would you help someone who was being cyber-bullied? What should be done to combat the problem?

TAKING IT TO THE WORD

Read Matthew 5:38–41

- These verses are quite hard to swallow. Why do you think Jesus says these things?

- What is the effect on others if you approach bullies in this way? How would people feel about you? How might they feel about the bullies?

- Could you give someone who was being bullied these verses? Why or why not?

SECTION D:
Talking movies

Introduction

There was a truly terrible advert on television around the time I wrote this, for the computer wholesaler PC World. The slogan was "my world is movies", the grammar of which slightly irked me, yet, I identified with the sentiment. There's something about the dazzle of the big screen which has totally captivated me, to the point that I stay obsessively up-to-date with the latest releases, the projects that various stars and directors have "in production", and even the rumours of the new ideas they might or might not be planning.

I am not alone – in fact there are many, many people who take this far more seriously than I do. The world is full of film fans – where centuries ago the theatre and fine art formed the centre-point of culture, now cinema screens (and often cinema-sized TV screens) are where the grand stories of our culture are played out.

For young people, film holds great appeal and always has done. Not only do they get to see their most fantastical dreams (and some of their favourite books!) on a giant canvas, they also get to explore ideas – and sometimes taboos – that they can't elsewhere.

Film is a brilliant springboard for discussion. I have used film in a number of ways with many young people, and it never fails to inspire, enthral, and create conversation. Speaking as a purist, I think the greatest impact can be seen when a group or individual takes time to watch a movie in it's entirety – as the storyteller intended – before sitting down to discuss it. Pragmatically, however, I know it's unrealistic to suggest this, unless you are working with a film club.

So, while some people are critical of an out-of-context approach to using film, this section includes 25 ready-to-use discussion starters, based around short movie clips which can be used to illustrate a key teaching or talking point. I have intentionally tried to ensure that none of these are used out of context from the rest of the film from which they are taken. Each make sense on their own, but the point they illustrate will still hold true if you go on to watch the movie as a whole.

In this section, only two banks of questions are supplied – the first around the clip itself, and the second around a relevant Bible passage. As ever, I suggest that you pick and choose from these as appropriate. These discussion starters could work well in a number of contexts – most notably small groups. Wherever you do use them, you will need to ensure you are acting in compliance with the law around copyright licensing. For more information on this, visit: www.ccli.org.uk.

A final disclaimer: the age ratings of these films range from U to 15. In all cases, I have chosen clips which do not contain excessive language, violence or sex – but that's not to say these elements aren't present in the full films. It's always a good idea to cue-up clips as precisely as possible (I have provided times to within a second or two) in order to avoid embarrassment, and if you are planning to watch the film with your group as a whole, it's important that you watch it on your own first to check for any possible "video nasties".

Some of the films listed are recent releases; others are old classics. All were available on DVD at time of writing.

D1

THEME: **Speaking up**

BIBLE: **Proverbs 31**

Stand up, speak out

Movie: *Changeling* (15)

Clip details: The clip begins after 13 minutes and 30 seconds. It runs for 1 minute and 50 seconds.

Synopsis: Influential Los Angeles minister, Reverend Gustav Briegleb, uses the opportunity of a sermon being broadcast on the radio to scathingly criticize the LAPD.

Summary

Based on a true story, *Changeling* is the sometimes-harrowing tale of Christine Collins (Angelina Jolie), a single mother living in 1920s Los Angeles, whose life is turned upside down when her nine-year-old son Walter disappears.

Though she isn't a churchgoer, Christine finds an ally in outspoken local churchman Gustav Briegleb (John Malkovich), who publicizes her plight from the pulpit and beyond, and uses the same platform to criticize the police department, which is rife with corruption. The unit is incompetent in the extreme, and totally compromised through its involvement in prostitution, gambling, and more; worst of all, its "gun squad" is acting totally above the law. When no one else is prepared to speak up for fear that it might make them a target, it is the Reverend who chooses to use his platform to do so.

As the movie continues, the LAPD attempt to restore their falling reputation by returning Christine's son, who they claim to have found alive. But when mother and son are "reunited", there's a shock – she's certain that this isn't the same boy. With the police insistent, Christine again has only one place to turn – and again Briegleb is there for her.

In this scene, Briegleb is using his Sunday sermon – which is also being broadcast on the radio across Los Angeles – to again show his concern for Christine, and then to rail against the police for their incompetence and corruption. He actually calls them "the most violent, corrupt and incompetent police department this side of the Rocky Mountains".

OPENING UP

- What kind of risks do you think the minister is taking by so publicly criticizing the police?

- Why do you think he has decided to do this? What might have motivated him?

- Do you think you would have the courage to speak up against the kind of corrupt institution that he seems to be describing?

- The Reverend tells his congregation that even though Christine isn't part of his church, they should still pray for her. What could all Christians learn from this?

TAKING IT TO THE WORD

Read Proverbs 31:8–9a

- Who around you "cannot speak for themselves"?

- What does it mean for you to "speak up" for them? Can you really do this? Why or why not?

- How can you practically "defend the rights of the poor and needy"? In your community? In the wider world?

- Commit to finding at least one way that you can respond to these commands in the week ahead.

D2

THEME: **Lasting love**

BIBLE: **Psalm 118**

Enduring love

Movie: *Juno* (12)

Clip details: The clip begins 1 hour, 17 minutes into the DVD. It runs for 3 minutes and 35 seconds.

Synopsis: With her naive view of love challenged, Juno seeks the truth on the subject from her flawed but ultimately loving dad.

Summary

Independently spirited, although studio produced, *Juno* was one of the surprise hits at the 2008 Oscars ceremony, where screenwriter Diablo Cody picked up the statue for Best Original Screenplay. Immensely popular among teenagers – especially those who would term themselves "alternative" – the film tells the simple story of quirky 16-year-old Juno Macguff (Ellen Page), whose world is turned upside down when she learns that she's pregnant.

After she and the child's father, Bleeker (Michael Cera) decide that they are too young to be parents, Juno chooses a seemingly perfect childless couple to adopt her baby. However, after meeting and initially falling for the charms of yuppies Mark and Vanessa, cracks soon begin to appear in their relationship, and Juno is left with a difficult decision about her baby.

In this scene, Juno has returned from discovering the truth about Mark and Vanessa's relationship. Emotional and heavily pregnant, Juno seeks out the advice of her father, a rough diamond of a man who has had good and bad experiences of love and marriage. Shaken by what she's learned, and wondering if she could ever make things work with Bleeker, Juno asks her dad if it's possible for two people to stay happy together forever.

Juno's dad replies that although he doesn't have the greatest track record, he's lasted ten happy years with Juno's stepmother. And he's philosophical, telling his daughter to: "find a person who loves you for exactly who you are". For Juno, who is "dealing with things way beyond my maturity level", these are just the words she needs to hear.

OPENING UP

- What would your answer be to Juno's question: "Can two people stay happy together forever?" What factors might influence your answer?

- What do you make of her dad's answer? Is this a good way to choose a boyfriend or girlfriend? What might the flaws in this argument be?

- What examples have you seen of truly lasting love? Why do you think these relationships work?

TAKING IT TO THE WORD

Read Psalm 118:1–8

- What do we learn about the nature of God's love in these verses?

- Why should these verses comfort us when people let us down?

- How well does this passage answer Juno's question, and tie in with her dad's response?

D3

THEME: **Free will**

BIBLE: **Psalm 139; Deuteronomy 30**

Free Will Ferrell

Movie: *Stranger than Fiction* (12)

Clip details: The clip begins 3 minutes and 55 seconds into the DVD. It runs for 3 minutes.

Synopsis: Harold begins to hear a voice in his head, accurately narrating his life.

Summary

Tax official Harold Crick (Will Ferrell) lives the blandest life imaginable. Every morning he brushes each of his teeth the same number of times, then takes the same number of steps to reach the same bus, to the same office, where he does the same things. His life is completely devoid of colour or shade; he has no real interests, few friends, and no one to love.

Everything changes, however, when Harold begins to hear a voice in his head. Initially, it's misdiagnosed as schizophrenia, but after enlisting the help of literature Professor Jules Hilbert (Dustin Hoffman), he ascertains that in fact it's the voice of a narrator. More than that – she's a real living author (played by Emma Thompson), and she's really about to complete work on a real book, called *Death and Taxes*. Harold is the main character, and everything she writes about him happens in real life. This would be fine, except that she's struggling with writer's block, desperately searching for a way to *kill Harold off*.

In this clip, Harold is brushing his teeth (the same number of times as usual) when suddenly, without explanation, he begins to hear the narrator's voice. It tells him, knowingly, that his life is dull – as others might be considering their hopes for the day or remembering their dreams, "Harold just counted brush strokes". As he gets ready, Harold realizes that as he deviates from his usual cast-iron routine, the voice stops. Then, when he returns to his usual processes, the voice continues again.

Is his life actually on rails? Is someone else pulling the strings? Harold Crick is extremely confused.

OPENING UP

- Instead of focusing on the joys of life, "Harold just counted brush strokes". Why do you think Harold does that? How do you feel about this character?

- Imagine that you were hearing an accurate narration of your life? How would it make you feel? How would you feel about the narrator?

- Do you see God in this way? Do you imagine that he knows every step you take? Do you think he controls it? Why or why not?

TAKING IT TO THE WORD

Read Psalm 139:1–16 and Deuteronomy 30:15–20

- These two passages tell us about two sides of God's relationship with the world. What are the two messages here?

- Do you think these contradict or complement each other? Explain your answer.

- After reading these verses, do you think God is more or less like the narrator in *Stranger than Fiction*? Why? What impact does all of this have on your life?

D4

THEME: **Standing up**

BIBLE: **Genesis 18**

When good men do something

Movie: *Valkyrie* (12)

Clip details: The clip starts after 32 minutes and 15 seconds. It runs for 2 minutes.

Synopsis: Tresckow tells Stauffenberg that their attempt to kill Adolf Hitler is bigger than any of them.

Summary

It's a hard sell – a movie where you know from the start that the heroes aren't successful. Yet, *Valkyrie* still manages to be incredibly powerful, and has important things to say about honour, integrity, and not standing silent in the face of evil.

Set towards the end of the Second World War, the film tells the true story of a failed attempt to assassinate Adolf Hitler by some of his own senior officers. Tom Cruise plays Claus Von Stauffenberg, a Catholic aristocrat and colonel in the German army who became involved in the "German Resistance" movement. The movement was made up of influential men in the military and political arena who agreed that Nazism had to be stopped, and their own leader overthrown.

Operation Valkyrie was a complex subversion of

an existing military strategy, in which the reserve army in Berlin would restore law and order in the event of heavy allied bombing. By getting Hitler to unwittingly sign a revised version of the strategy, Stauffenberg had changed the plan into a way of overthrowing the Nazis – as long as Hitler could be separately assassinated – by Stauffenberg himself.

In this scene, Stauffenberg is receiving a pep talk from his co-conspirator, Major-General Henning von Tresckow (Kenneth Branagh). As Stauffenberg tries to work out who he can trust, his friend advises him to have confidence only in his own integrity: "God promised Abraham that he would not destroy Sodom if he could find ten righteous men... I have a feeling that for Germany it may come down to one."

OPENING UP

- When you think of Germany in the early 1940s, do you imagine everyone was behind Hitler? Why or why not?

- How do you think you might have behaved and acted if you had been born into this society? Would you have stood up against the flow?

- What do you think was behind von Tresckow's warning?

TAKING IT TO THE WORD

Read Genesis 18:20–33. Also paraphrase what happened to Sodom (see 19:23–29), and explain Sodom's sin (see Ezekiel 16:49).

- Why do you think in a city of thousands, not even ten people were leading good and just lives?

- What experience have you had of seeing others – or yourself

– going along with the crowd? Why did this happen?

- Pray together that you will be people who stand up for justice and righteousness, even when everyone around you is doing something else.

D5

THEME: **Repentance**

BIBLE: **Acts 3**

Repent!

Movie: *There Will Be Blood* (15)

Clip details: The clip begins 1 hour, 47 minutes and 30 seconds into the DVD. It runs for 4 minutes exactly.

Synopsis: Oil baron Daniel Plainview is forced to repent of his sins by a crazed preacher, in front of the whole community.

Summary

One of the great films of the last decade, *There Will Be Blood* is the epic story of "oil man" Daniel Plainview, an independent prospector who builds an empire with his bare hands at the turn of the twentieth century. Daniel Day Lewis gives an extraordinary, Oscar-winning performance as Plainview, a man whose sanity slowly begins to disintegrate in the face of his insatiable ambition for power.

Plainview's adversary is a man of faith, the strange and youthful preacher Eli Sunday. Their battle of wits spans the length of the film, and as they struggle for supremacy in the small community, the fight inevitably drags them both down.

When Plainview is told that he can only run a pipeline through a local farm if he converts in Eli's church, the preacher spots an opportunity to publicly defeat his rival. In this clip, Plainview is hauled to the stage and receives a verbal and physical battering, enduring every kind of abuse in order to be able to build his pipeline. Most cruelly, Eli forces him to admit that he has abandoned his deaf son by sending him to live at a special school. "I've abandoned my child!" he roars, knowing the truth in that statement, and hating Eli all the more for forcing it out of him.

OPENING UP

- Where do you think God is in this scene? Is Plainview really "saving" himself through this experience? Why or why not?

- What do you think Plainview is thinking as he makes his confession?

- What do you think Plainview whispers to Eli after the baptism?

- How does this clip help you to consider how we communicate the gospel? The mistakes we can make?

TAKING IT TO THE WORD

Read Acts 3:17–20

- How do these words contrast with Eli's view of "conversion" and "repentance"? How does the language differ?

- What do we learn here about the nature of true repentance?

- How do you respond personally to these words?

D6

THEME: **Life choices**

BIBLE: **1 Samuel 17**

Man versus giant

Movie: *Transformers* (12)

Clip details: The clip begins 52 minutes and 40 seconds into the DVD. It runs for 1 minute and 45 seconds.

Synopsis: A robot transforms into a car, then it invites Sam and Mikaela to step inside.

Summary

Like, I suspect, many children of the 1980s, this writer was thrilled when the *Transformers* live-action movie was announced. The chance to see the most popular toys of my youth realized as 100-foot CGI monsters on the big screen was a pretty attractive prospect, and while the plot and acting don't exactly evoke *Citizen Kane*, Michael Bay's film is exactly what it needs to be to satisfy the fans: big, visceral, and exceedingly loud.

The story isn't terribly important, but surrounds young Sam Witwicky (Shia Leboeuf), who unknowingly possesses the key to the most powerful weapon in the universe. An Autobot (one of the good Transformers) named Bumblebee is sent to protect Sam, but can't prevent him from being thrust into the centre of a war between the Autobots and their evil enemies, the

Decepticons, which could result in the destruction of the Earth itself.

In this scene, Sam and his beautiful former classmate Mikaela (Megan Fox) have just discovered that Sam's new car is in fact a giant transforming robot. After witnessing a battle between it (Bumblebee) and a Decepticon, the former turns back into a car, and opens a door invitingly to the two shell-shocked young people. Mikaela isn't sure, but Sam is fearlessly philosophical. He knows that this is a decision that could alter the direction of his life: "Fifty years from now, when you're looking back at your life, don't you want to be able to say you had the guts to get in the car?"

OPENING UP

- Do you think you would get in the car? Why or why not?

- What does Sam mean when he talks about looking back on his life?

- Fifty years from now, what kind of life would you like to have lived?

TAKING IT TO THE WORD

Read 1 Samuel 17:1–49 (you may want to paraphrase the first half)

- What similarities do you see between this story and the clip?

- What implications would David's decision to fight Goliath have had on his future?

- How did David arrive at this seemingly crazy decision (verses 34–37)?

- If you make big decisions on the same basis as David, what kind of life do you think you will live?

D7

THEME: **Spiritual gifts**

BIBLE: **1 Corinthians 14**

Prophecy!

Movie: *The Simpsons Movie* (PG)

Clip details: The clip begins 4 minutes into the DVD. It runs for 3 minutes.

Synopsis: When Grandpa Simpson has an apparent prophetic revelation from God his family are so embarrassed that they drag him away from church.

Summary

One of the most interesting aspects of the world's most popular and best-loved animated TV series is that it takes place within a Christian paradigm. Extraordinarily the plot of this big-screen version is kicked off by a moment that only makes sense within that context: as God is invited to speak through a church congregation, and apparently does so through the shrivelled and often-ignored Grandpa Simpson.

The sudden touch of God is enough to provoke a violent physical reaction from Grandpa, who makes such a commotion that one character even begins filming him on a camera phone. Embarrassed, Grandpa's family bundle him outside in a rolled-up carpet, but not before he has shouted a number of (what later prove to be dead-accurate) prophetic messages.

In the car outside, our sort-of hero Homer wants to bury the experience and go for waffles, but his long-suffering wife Marge is reluctant to comply. "What is the point in going to church every Sunday," she asks, "when if someone we love has a genuine religious experience, we ignore it?"

OPENING UP

- Which of the characters' reactions might best reflect your own response to such an experience? Would you film it all on your camera phone, take it seriously, or go for waffles? Why?

- Do you believe God speaks through people today? If so, how?

- Has God ever spoken to you? What happened?

TAKING IT TO THE WORD

Read 1 Corinthians 14:1–5

- What are spiritual gifts? Do you believe they are still available today?

- What does Paul say about prophecy and tongues here? What can we learn?

- Why might God connect with people in these ways?

- If appropriate, you could ask God to speak to you, right now. Spend some time in silence, and listen to him.

D8

THEME:　**Unrequited love**

BIBLE:　**Ezekiel 16**

◆ Different kinds of love

Movie: *The Holiday* (12)

Clip details: The clip starts 1 minute after the studio logo appears at the beginning. It runs for 2 minutes and 35 seconds. You should try to end it as soon as Kate Winslet's opening monologue ends, as there is some mild bad language immediately afterwards.

Synopsis: Iris presents her views of the different kinds of love.

Summary

In *The Holiday*, Iris (Kate Winslet) is terminally unlucky in love. She's been in love with the wrong man for three years, and now she's about to find out that he's marrying someone else. Her unhappiness then leads her to jump into a risky house swap with Amanda (Cameron Diaz), a woman she meets online. Amanda spends Christmas in Iris' home in Surrey, while Iris spends the same time living in Los Angeles. The swap isn't without its difficulties, but in the end both women find love and meaning in these temporary homes.

In this clip from the start of the movie, Iris is at her office Christmas party, back in England. As the camera shows us a number of the main characters we are about to meet, Iris reflects on the different kinds of love between people: true love, love that fades, love that is lost, sex, and unrequited love. It is that last kind of love which sums up Iris' position. She has been in love with Jasper for years, and yet, she knows that he will never love her back.

Iris says that unrequited love has been responsible for some of the unhappiest times of her life. Now she faces another Christmas, unhappy, alone, and thinking of the man she loves, but who does not love her.

OPENING UP

- Which of the different kinds of love in Iris' monologue do you identify with?

- What other kinds of love can you think of? What do you think are the best and worst kinds of love?

- What do you understand by the phrase "unrequited love"? Have you experienced it? How did it make you feel?

- How have you experienced the love of others?

- How have you experienced the love of God?

TAKING IT TO THE WORD

Read Ezekiel 16:9–22

- In this fairly graphic passage, God is speaking through a prophet to his people Israel in a metaphorical picture. What do you think this is really about? Is this really about prostitution?

- What do you know about the Old Testament story, and how does that help you to understand this passage?

- What do we learn about God's character from this passage?

- This is a description of how God's love for man was thrown back in his face – a kind of unrequited love. What does this then say to us about God's decision to send Jesus?

- Is God's love unrequited today? If so, how? If not, why not?

- Do you think you "love" God? Explain your answer.

D9

THEME: **Honouring parents**

BIBLE: **Ephesians 6**

Perfect parents?

Movie: *Coraline* (PG)

Clip details: The clip starts after 14 minutes and 15 seconds. It runs for 4 minutes.

Synopsis: Coraline is reminded of her parents' shortcomings over dinner, but then a strange door opens up and leads her to a new mum and dad...

Summary

Coraline is the weirdly wonderful stop-motion movie adaptation of Neil Gaiman's fantasy novel. It tells the story of Coraline Jones, a young girl who moves with her family to a new house – hundreds of miles from the place where she grew up. Her new home is an apartment in a mysterious mansion, a building full of hiding places and secrets.

One of these secrets is a small door, hidden away out of sight, which Coraline pesters her mother to unlock. When she does so – on the understanding that her daughter is then silent – there are apparently only bricks behind it. Soon, however, the doorway is revealed to be much more interesting...

In this clip, Coraline eats dinner with her

dysfunctional parents – neither of whom show much in the way of care or affection for her. They are selfish and preoccupied by their own importance, feed her inedible mush, and treat her with contempt. That night, Coraline retreats sadly to sleep, but she is quickly disturbed by a visitor from the secret door.

This time, when she returns to the door, Coraline finds that the brick wall has been replaced by a strange corridor. On the other side she finds an almost exact replica of her house – but on this side, everything is different. The ugly picture from her house has been replaced with one much more attractive; the bleak rooms she is used to are flooded with light and life.

In the kitchen, Coraline's mother is singing and cooking – two things she would never do on the other side of the door. And in the study, her father greets her with a song that he has written just for her. On this side of the door, Coraline's life is filled with love, laughter, and joy. Or, so it seems. But why is it that on this side, her parents have buttons sewn over their eyes...?

OPENING UP

- On which side of the tunnel do you think you would feel safer or happier? Why?

- Do you think Coraline's regular parents are mean, or just busy? Can you understand why they behave in this way?

- Which of these pictures of parenting is more realistic to you? Why?

TAKING IT TO THE WORD

Read Ephesians 6:1–4

- How does the Bible explain the responsibilities for parents and children?

- How might these verses apply to the characters in *Coraline*?

- Why would honouring your parents mean you lived a long life?

- When do your parents "exasperate" you? Are there ways you can avoid exasperating them?

D10

THEME: **Death**

BIBLE: **John 11**

Before I die...

Movie: *The Bucket List* (12)

Clip details: The clip begins 47 minutes and 10 seconds into the DVD. It runs for 2 minutes and 20 seconds.

Synopsis: Carter explains his belief in a creator to atheist Edward as they fly over Nepal.

Summary

What would you do if you knew you had six months to live? How would you spend your final days on earth? These are the questions posed by *The Bucket List*, the story of two men who find themselves in exactly that situation.

The two main characters have both been diagnosed with terminal cancer. Billionaire Edward (a perfectly cast Jack Nicholson) has no family to leave his fortune to, but poor car mechanic Carter (a suitably sympathetic Morgan Freeman) has little wealth but a loving family. Edward invites Carter to join him on a last pilgrimage, on which they will live life to the fullest. They create a list of things they would like to do and see before they "kick the bucket" (die) and then set about ticking off the list, courtesy of Edward's unlimited financial resources.

As they begin to tick off the achievements, their

thoughts inevitably turn toward questions of death, and what comes next. At the same time, Edward realizes that, while he's financially the far richer man, he's actually poor compared to Carter, who enjoys the priceless love of a close family.

In this clip, Edward and Carter are on a plane from America to Nepal, where they are going to tick a visit to Mount Everest off the "Bucket List". Struck by the awesomeness of the night sky, Carter reveals his faith in a creator to his bemused companion. The two men then reveal that they are facing death in very different ways – one of them full of hope, the other simply expecting to expire.

OPENING UP

- What do you want to see or do before you die? Why?

- About the afterlife, Edward says: "I'd love to be wrong. If I'm wrong, I win!" What would you say to him?

- What do you think of Edward's claim that 95 per cent of the people on earth are wrong about God?

TAKING IT TO THE WORD

Read John 11:17–26

- This is the story of Jesus' visit to the home of a dead man. How does his talk of life and death take on two meanings? (You might want to read on to find out more!)

- What is your answer to Jesus' question in verse 26? What does this even mean?

- How much do you think about your own death? How do Jesus' words in these verses comfort or concern you?

D11

THEME: **Redemption**

BIBLE: **Matthew 27**

Turning it around

Movie: *Blades of Glory* (12)

Clip details: The clip begins 23 minutes and 25 seconds into the movie. It lasts for 1 minute.

Synopsis: A figure skating coach spots the potential for the perfect partnership… as he watches two disgraced former stars fighting.

Summary

Blades of Glory is a "frat-pack" comedy set in the world of competitive figure skating. Will Ferrell plays champion skater Chazz Michael Michaels, who brawls with his arch-rival Jimmy MacElroy (Jon Heder) after they tie for a gold medal at the world championships. The fight sends shockwaves through the sport, and the pair are banned for life from the men's competition.

After being wrenched from their true calling, both men quickly spiral into despair. Jimmy is disowned by his father and takes a job fitting skates, while Chazz turns to alcohol as he takes a part in children's ice spectacular *Grublets on Ice*. But when MacElroy realizes that he can still compete in the pairs' competition, he instructs his coach (Craig T. Nelson) to find him a partner.

The coach doesn't find MacElroy the kind of partner he was expecting, however, and teams him up with his nemesis, Micheals. Together, the pair "fight" against the odds to compete together in the world championships, and even learn to like and respect each other along the way.

In this clip, the coach watches a TV news report, detailing a fight in the backstage area of Michaels' children's show *Grublets on Ice*. The fight involves Michaels and MacElroy, who the coach trained for many years. As the coach watches the footage closely, however, he realizes that as the two are throwing each other around, they are doing so with the kind of grace and creativity normally only seen on the ice rink. At once he realizes – Micheals and MacElroy shouldn't be fighting – they should be skating together!

OPENING UP

- What does the coach see in the TV footage, that everyone else has missed? Why do you think he spots it?

- How might he respond next? What might prevent the coach from acting on what he has seen?

- Have you ever seen a seemingly negative situation turned around for good? What happened? What was the driving force in the change?

- What does the word "redemption" mean to you (maybe look it up)?

- What other movies or stories can you think of where this idea of redemption is illustrated? What happens?

TAKING IT TO THE WORD

Read Matthew 27:45–54

- This appears to be the lowest point in human history – but what's really going on here? What do the strange goings-on in verses 51–53 suggest about Jesus and his death?

- How is the centurion like the coach in *Blades of Glory*? What do you think he will do next?

- How is this a "redemptive" story?

- How do you think the other onlookers responded? How do you respond to this story?

D12

THEME: **Justice fatigue**

BIBLE: **Matthew 23**

Go on eating your dinner

Movie: *Hotel Rwanda* (15)

Clip Details: The clip begins after 42 minutes and 10 seconds. It lasts for 2 minutes and 20 seconds.

Synopsis: Paul thinks the video footage that has been captured of the Rwandan massacre will make the world sit up and take notice.

Summary

Hotel Rwanda is a partly true story set in the midst of the horrors of the Rwandan genocides of the 1990s. Unspeakable acts of mass violence were committed by the Hutu tribe against hundreds of thousands of members of the Tutsi tribe.

As the violence between the two tribes escalated to the point where Tutsis were being murdered by the Hutu militia, many Tutsi civilians retreated into the hotel where Paul Rusesabagina (Don Cheadle), a Hutu with a Tutsi wife, was assistant manager.

Through Paul's intervention, in allowing over a thousand Tutsis to take refuge in his hotel, he was able to save many lives that might otherwise have been taken by the rampaging militiamen. When all around – especially the UN peacekeepers led by Colonel Oliver (Nick Nolte) – were failing the Tutsi people, Paul became an unlikely, and at times unwilling, hero.

In this clip, an American film crew have captured graphic footage of the genocide going on in Rwanda. At last, there is proof that the long-rumoured acts of despicable violence in the country are truly taking place. Paul feels great relief, and believes that at last the outside world will hear the cry of the persecuted Hutu people.

Journalist Jack Dalglish (Joaquin Phoenix) is less sure, however. His cynicism is shocking both to Paul and to us. "How can [the world] not intervene when they witness such atrocities?" asks Paul. Jack's jaded reply is deeply discouraging: "I think if people see this footage, they'll say, 'Oh my God, that's horrible,' and then go on eating their dinners."

OPENING UP

- What do you know about the Rwandan genocide? If a lot, how did you find out? If a little, why do you think this is the case (over a million people died)?

- Who do you agree with in this scene? Jack, with his cynical view of human nature, or Paul, who is more idealistic?

- If Jack is right, what are some of the reasons for the "justice fatigue" that people seem to feel?

- How could we start to address this problem?

TAKING IT TO THE WORD

Read Matthew 23:23

- There is a lot of content in this one verse! What is Jesus' accusation regarding the Pharisees?

- Why does he bring up their giving? How does that translate to the way we can sometimes view charity and giving today?

- Would someone with a true passion for "justice, mercy and faithfulness" be able to "go on eating their dinner"? Why or why not?

- James 2:14–17 talks about how "faith without works is dead". Pray together that God will help you to understand this truth fully – without allowing you to become unbalanced in your faith.

D13

THEME: **The end of the world**

BIBLE: **1 Thessalonians 4**

Armageddon outta here!

Movie: *The Hitchhiker's Guide to the Galaxy* (PG)

Clip details: The clip can be located 10 minutes, 48 seconds into the DVD. It runs for 3 minutes, 12 seconds, and should end as the Earth explodes.

Synopsis: Alien Ford Prefect's wild claims about the end of the world are proved true.

Summary

Arthur Dent (Martin Freeman) is having a very bad day. His house is about to be demolished, and his best friend Ford (Mos Def) keeps banging on about Armageddon. In the local pub, bemused residents ask what they should do in the event that his prediction is correct. "Shouldn't we lie down with a paper bag over our heads?" asks the worried barman.

Leaving the pub, after Ford has generously bought everyone a final drink, Arthur discovers that his house has been torn down. His rage is short-lived, however, when a giant spaceship appears above them. On board, a hideous alien civil engineer announces that, true to Ford's prediction, the Earth is to be demolished immediately to make way for a new hyperspace bypass.

As the multitudes on Earth realize their fate,

widespread panic breaks out, except in the ruins of Arthur's house, where Ford thumbs for an intergalactic lift, and the pub, where everyone lies down with paper bags on their heads. Moments later, the camera pans back to take in the devastating scale of the Vogon constructor fleet, which quickly reduces the planet to dust and ash.

OPENING UP

- Describe the different reactions you saw to the end of the world. Which kind of reaction do you think you would have displayed?

- Do you worry about the end of the world? Why or why not? If so, describe your fears.

- How do you think the world will end? What do you think the Bible says?

TAKING IT TO THE WORD

Read 1 Thessalonians 4:13–18

- This is the end of the world as the Bible describes it. How does it compare to and fit in with your own theories about Armageddon?

- What do you think it will mean to "meet the Lord in the air"?

- What does this passage also say about people who have died before the Lord comes? Why do you think the dead will rise before the living?

- Is this what you thought the Bible would say on this subject? If not, what did you expect?

- What do you need to do to make sure you spend eternity with God? Do you feel confident that you will?

D14

THEME: **Sexual abstinence**

BIBLE: **1 Thessalonians 4**

It's called "making love", isn't it?

Movie: *17 Again* (12)

Clip details: The clip starts after 44 minutes and 40 seconds. It runs for 3 minutes (you may wish to stop the clip before the fight at the end).

Synopsis: Trapped inside a teenager's body, 30-something Mike has a different perspective on sex and abstinence.

Summary

With teen pin-up Zac Efron as its star, *17 Again* was always going to be a smash hit movie. Yet, despite being another trawl through a very well-worn movie plot, it still manages to find something meaningful to say to its teenage audience.

At 17, Mike O'Donnell (played at this age by Efron) had it all – a beautiful girlfriend, big dreams, and an exciting future. Yet, somehow it all went wrong, and now in his mid-30s (played by *Friends* star Matthew Perry) he finds himself at rock bottom. One night though, with his life in pieces, Mike falls off a bridge – and when he wakes up, he's Zac Efron!

Having been granted a second chance, Mike

enrols in the same school he attended two decades earlier, assumes the new name "Mark", and sets about attempting to rebuild his family.

In this scene, Mike/Mark sits through a health education class run by a teacher who seems to have a very cynical view of teenage sexuality. Although the official school policy is to promote abstinence, she clearly believes this is an unrealistic expectation. Having the benefit of hindsight, Mike knows that sexual promiscuity isn't all it's cracked up to be, and expects to find an ally in this teacher. When he realizes that he will find no support from her, he decides to take matters into his own hands.

The speech he delivers – which sounds a bit ridiculous coming from a teenage mouth – is a stirring defence of "making love" instead of having sex, based on his experiences of having had – and lost – a true loving relationship.

OPENING UP

- What are your feelings about Mike's speech? What were some of his beliefs – were they right? Realistic?

- Teenagers are often portrayed as sex mad – so did you believe some of the reactions to his words?

- Do you believe you could influence people in your school on sex if you had Mike's courage? Why or why not?

TAKING IT TO THE WORD

Read 1 Thessalonians 4:1–8

- These might seem like quite negative verses – telling people not to commit sexual sin. What might be some positive reasons behind this instruction?

- What does it mean to control your own body? Is that a state of mind, a daily decision, or something else?

- 1 Corinthians 7:2–3 (and if you are prepared for a bit of giggling, Proverbs 5:18–19) makes clear that sex – is of God. Why do you think the church sometimes doesn't represent that? How could we get better at talking honestly and positively about sex?

D15

THEME: **Deceit**

BIBLE: **Genesis 12**

A lie worth telling?

Movie: *King Kong* (12)

Clip details: The clip can be located at 19 minutes and 45 seconds. It runs for 3 minutes and 15 seconds.

Synopsis: Denham tricks Jack into staying on his ship until it leaves port.

Summary

At the start of blockbuster adventure movie *King Kong*, no one yet knows that the giant ape of the title even exists. All movie director Carl Denham (Jack Black) is concerned about is getting a cast and crew on to a boat bound for the mysterious and uncharted Skull Island. Unfortunately, the movie studios have lost faith in him, and refuse to finance his trip. Desperate and determined to still make his movie, Denham gets his boat ready to leave anyway.

Key to the success of Denham's movie is the presence of hotshot screenwriter Jack Driscoll (Adrien Brody). In this clip, he is delivering the first portion of the script to Denham, on his boat. To Denham's dismay, Jack has only written a handful of pages – nowhere near enough for Denham to start shooting. He apologizes, but says that he's been very busy, and now needs to leave the boat to get back to work in the theatre. Now the pressure is really mounting: Denham has no money and no script, and the police, alerted by the studios, are on his tail!

Denham can see that the boat is beginning to leave port, and decides to trick Jack into remaining on board until it's too late. He offers him a cheque, paying for his work, but repeatedly messes it up on purpose. Jack gives up and makes for the exit, but the boat has pulled away, leaving him trapped on board and bound for Skull Island. Through several tricks like this, Denham has managed to escape the clutches of the studios and the police, and has somehow departed with a full cast and crew.

OPENING UP

- Is Denham's behaviour actually lying? Or something else?

- With all the pressure on his head, do you understand why Denham tricked Jack? Is he justified?

- How do you think Jack feels when he realizes what has happened?

- What might be the consequences of Denham's deceit?

TAKING IT TO THE WORD

Read Genesis 12:10–20

- Why does Abraham deceive the Egyptians? Do you think he was right to do so?

- What do you think were the consequences of Abraham's deceit – for him; for the Egyptians; for Sarai; for their marriage?

- He seems to get away with it – yet, in the story of Ananias and Sapphira (Acts 5:1–11), God punishes liars with death. Why do you think the two outcomes are so different?

- Are lies and deceit ever justifiable? Explain your answer.

D16

THEME: **Change**
BIBLE: **Exodus 4**

Change the world

Movie: *Ratatouille* (U)

Clip details: The clip begins 59 minutes and 30 seconds into the DVD. It runs for 1 minute and 30 seconds.

Synopsis: Remy the rat refuses to believe his father when he says that they can't change the status quo.

Summary

Ratatouille might be a cartoon (or more accurately, a digital animation), but its themes will pack a punch with all generations. The movie follows the story of Remy, a food-loving rat from provincial France who finds himself washed up in the drains of Paris, and is soon following his extraordinary dream of becoming a chef. Considering the difficult relationship between rats and kitchens, this seems an unlikely goal, until Remy meets Linguini, a bottom-rung worker in the city's finest restaurant.

After realizing their mutual love of food, they set out to work together to become a formidable cooking team. At first (since they can't speak the same language) it seems impossible, but when Remy realizes that he can control Linguini like a puppet by pulling his hair, they begin to win over staff and customers at the restaurant with their amazing culinary skills.

Remy suffers a knock-back, however, when he is reunited with his family. Remy's father, Django, is a brutal realist, and tells his son that he can't trust humans. To illustrate his point, in this clip he takes his son to a nearby exterminator's shop, the window of which is gruesomely decorated with the corpses of dead rats – many with their heads still clamped in traps.

Django tells his son that "this is the way things are; you can't change nature". Remy isn't sure, however. He believes that "change is nature", and with renewed determination, sets off to prove it.

OPENING UP

- Which statement do you agree most with: "you can't change nature", or "change is nature"? Why?

- Why do you think many people fear change?

- If you could change one thing in your school or community, what would it be? What about bringing a change to your country? To the world?

TAKING IT TO THE WORD

Read Exodus 4:1–13 (summarize chapter 3 first)

- What is Moses' response to God's incredible plan to change the world?

- Why do you think Moses protests so much? How might this link with how many people fear change and new things?

- How can you trust God more in your dreams and plans to bring change in your local community – and beyond?

D17

THEME: **Relationships**

BIBLE: **Proverbs 4, 13 and 22**

◆ Girls love skills

Movie: *Napoleon Dynamite* (PG)

Clip details: The clip begins 33 minutes and 30 seconds into the DVD. It runs for 1 minute and 20 seconds.

Synopsis: Napoleon and Pedro discuss who they will take to the school dance.

Summary

Napoleon Dynamite's quirky heart makes it an ideal movie to watch in full, and doing so can give you the opportunity to draw out discussion on issues such as identity, self-confidence, friendship, and fitting in. If you have only got time for a clip, however, this one offers a fun way in to the tricky subject of teenage relationships.

Napoleon (Jon Heder) is the ultimate misfit – only saved by the fact that he doesn't realize it. Geeky and weird, and with a family that's even more so, Napoleon sees his mundane life as an adventure, and shares it with weasel-like brother Kip and best friend Pedro, "the only kid in school who can grow a moustache".

Fuelled by hormones, and despite unmanageable hair, both boys decide that the big thing missing from their lives is a girl, especially with the school dance looming. Pedro has already received a positive response from Napoleon's friend Deb, and now it's time for Napoleon to identify an object for his affections.

In this scene, Pedro and Napoleon discuss how to win a woman over, and Napoleon outlines his belief that girls "only want boyfriends who have great skills"! Pedro suggests that he should find a nice girl, draw a picture of her, and give it to her in order to win her heart. Napoleon thinks it's a great idea, and sets off in pursuit of his yearbook, to identify a suitable muse.

OPENING UP

- Are Pedro and Napoleon right about what women want? How successful do you think Napoleon's plan will be?

- How do you make decisions about who you want to go out with?

- Why do you think we go out with people in our teenage years? What does it achieve?

TAKING IT TO THE WORD

Read the following Proverbs 4:23, 13:20, and 22:24–25

- What does the first proverb tell us about how we should approach relationships?

- How can you "guard your heart" in practice?

- Do you think society would tell you to guard your heart, or take risks with it? Why?

- What do the last two proverbs tell us about who we should and shouldn't date?

- How would you translate the advice in these three proverbs into relationship advice for your friends – or even for Pedro and Napoleon?

D18

THEME: **Disappointment**

BIBLE: **James 1**

◆ Unanswered prayer

Movie: *Rescue Dawn* (12)

Clip details: The clip begins 1 hour, 34 minutes into the DVD. It runs for 3 minutes and 45 seconds.

Synopsis: Dieter's prayers go seemingly unanswered, as he attempts to escape the island where he has been held prisoner.

Summary

In the midst of the Vietnam War, US Navy pilot Dieter Dengler (Christian Bale) is shot down and captured by ruthless soldiers in Laos, over which he has been flying a top-secret mission. Taken to a Prisoner of War camp, he meets a group of other inmates, all of whom have lost hope, and many of whom are losing their grip on reality. Accompanied by Duane (Steve Zahn), Dieter eventually escapes the camp, but then has to find a way of somehow navigating his way out of enemy territory.

In this clip, with his spirits almost sapped by his journey through the cruel jungle, Dieter hears the buzzing of US helicopters overhead. His hopes rise as they approach, but are then dashed as they continue past, unable to spot him against the backdrop of thick undergrowth. That night, he sits with Duane, whose mind is rapidly failing him, and prays: "God, why don't you help us when we need you most?"

The next day, Dieter rises early to create a signal fire to attract the helicopters. It looks as if his prayers have been answered as they return, but to Dieter's shock, they mistake him for an enemy soldier and open fire on him. Lying face down in the mud, Dieter realizes his hopes have been dashed.

Note: Although the movie as a whole contains some bad language and moderate violence, you might consider using the entire film as a discussion starter on issues of hope, courage, and endurance.

OPENING UP

- What do you think Dieter felt when the helicopters ignored him? What about when they shot at him?

- If you were Dieter, what would you do next?

- Dieter prays: "God, why don't you help us when we need you most?" How would you respond to him?

TAKING IT TO THE WORD

Read James 1:2–8

- What do these verses tell us about dealing with our disappointments?

- How easy or difficult do you find it to persevere in tough times? Why is it important to persevere?

- Thinking back to the movie – do you think God will answer Dieter's prayer in the end? Why or why not?

D19

THEME: **Wisdom**

BIBLE: **1 Corinthians 1–2**

The right kind of wisdom

Movie: *Indiana Jones and the Last Crusade* (PG)

Clip details: For a longer clip, run from chapter 33 to the end, or for a shorter clip, from 1 hour 42 minutes and 45 seconds into the movie, for 1 minute and 45 seconds.

Synopsis: Indy must exercise great wisdom to pass four challenges and stay alive.

Summary

A classic clip now, as swashbuckling archaeologist Indiana Jones (Harrison Ford) nears the end of his quest for the Holy Grail. But just as he is getting close, evil Nazi Walter Donovan appears, shooting Indy's father Henry (Sean Connery) and sending our hero in to fetch the sought-after artefact. The grail is said to give immortality to anyone who drinks it – and now Indy needs its power to save his dad's life.

But there's a big problem. The grail is protected by three elaborate booby traps, which have been dispatching potential grave robbers to their doom for 700 years. Henry has spent years working out how to overcome them, and now Indy only has his father's scribbled notes to help him to negotiate a path fraught with danger.

Amid the appropriate amount of tension, Indy finds the wisdom to overcome each of the three challenges, and enters the room in which the grail is stored, guarded by a 750-year-old knight. There's a final deadly test though – the room is littered with cups with which to scoop up the holy water, and only one grants eternal life. The rest, as Walter Donovan discovers, bring death. Here, we see the wisdom of this world made to look foolish, as Indy shows true wisdom in recognizing "the cup of a carpenter".

OPENING UP

- What examples of wisdom did you see in the clip? How and why do they show wisdom?

- Put yourself in Indy's shoes – would you have made the same choices?

- Where does Indy get his wisdom from?

TAKING IT TO THE WORD

Read 1 Corinthians 1:18 – 2:10

- What is the difference between worldly wisdom and God's wisdom?

- What benefits could "becoming wise" have on your life?

- Think about some of the choices you have to make in your life. What might be a wise choice in those situations?

- How can you gain more of the right kind of wisdom? (Look at Proverbs 2:1–4 for some ideas.)

D20

THEME: **Revenge**

BIBLE: **Romans 12**

Unforgiven

Movie: *The Painted Veil* (12)

Clip details: The clip begins 23 minutes into the DVD. It runs for 5 minutes.

Synopsis: In 1920s China, young doctor Walter reacts to his wife's adultery by taking her to a remote village ravaged by a deadly epidemic.

Summary

The Painted Veil is a period epic based on a classic novel by W. Somerset Maugham, which tells the story of Walter (Edward Norton), a middle-class English doctor in the 1920s, and Kitty (Naomi Watts), the upper-class woman who married him for the wrong reasons. Kitty doesn't love Walter, but she is desperate to escape her overbearing family, and so uses him as an escape mechanism. The couple relocate to China, where Walter works as a bacteriologist, and Kitty experiences true love, albeit with another man, Charlie (Liev Schreiber).

When Walter uncovers the truth about Kitty and Charlie's affair, he takes drastic and vengeful action. In this clip, he calmly explains to Kitty that he has accepted a call to work in a remote Chinese village that has been ravaged by a terrible outbreak of deadly cholera – and that he intends to take her with him. She is horrified, especially as it would mean leaving her true love Charlie behind.

Desperate, she tells her husband that she will not go with him – but there's a terrible twist: Walter knows all about the affair. In fact, that's why he's accepted this near-suicidal job offer. He is so consumed by rage at his wife's infidelity, he's prepared to send them both into a situation that will probably cause each of them a painful death. He delivers his final threat – if she will not go with him, then he will divorce her publicly, citing adultery as a cause – the greatest humiliation that could be brought on someone of her social class. Now she must choose: total shame, or likely death...

OPENING UP

- What do you think Kitty will choose to do? What might you do if you were living in her situation and society, where divorce brings great shame?

- Do you understand Walter's actions? How else might he have reacted?

- What examples of revenge and "unforgiveness" can you think of, in the news, and elsewhere? In other stories, movies, etc.? Among your friends or school?

TAKING IT TO THE WORD

Read Romans 12:17–21

- How realistic do you think these commands are? Could you see yourself acting in this way to your "enemies"? Why or why not?

- What examples have you seen of "overcoming evil with good"?

- In the movie, how might Walter have responded to Kitty if he had followed this advice?

- These verses come in the context of a wider passage about love. What might that tell us about love?

D21

THEME: **Faith**

BIBLE: **Hebrews 11**

The invisible kingdom

Movie: *Stardust* (PG)

Clip details: The clip begins 40 seconds into the DVD. It runs for 2 minutes and 40 seconds.

Synopsis: Dunstan's faith in an invisible kingdom, hidden behind an ancient English wall, kick-starts an incredible adventure.

Summary

It's the mid-nineteenth century, and young Dunstan Thorn (Ben Barnes) lives in the uneventful English village of Wall. The village is so called because there's a seldom-crossed walled boundary between the settlement and the fields beyond it. In this clip, Dunstan approaches the only gap in the wall, where he's met by a guard (David Kelly), who refuses his request to pass through.

The guard tells him that this isn't just a gap in a wall, but a portal to another world, which has been under permanent 24-hour guard for hundreds of years. Dunstan secretly believes him, but tries to convince the guard that his claim is ridiculous. "Do you see another world out there?" he asks rhetorically. "No, you see a field!" The guard is resolute, but when he's caught, er... off-guard, Dunstan sprints past him and through the gap. His risk is soon rewarded, as we see that the secret world really does exist.

What follows is a tale of fallen stars, magic, and love, but it's Dunstan's faith that kicks it all off. Without his belief in something unseen, the adventure simply would never have got started.

OPENING UP

- Why do you think Dunstan believes there's something on the other side of the wall?

- Why is it important that he follows his convictions?

- What obstacles are there between you and the things you believe in?

TAKING IT TO THE WORD

Read Hebrews 11 (you might want to summarize the middle section)
- What does this passage tell us about the nature of faith?

- Focus particularly on verse 1. What do you hope for, and how sure are you of it?

- What would or wouldn't you do for something you believed, but didn't "know" for sure? Where do you draw the line? Could you give up your time? Your money? Your life?

D22

THEME: **Gifts and talents**

BIBLE: **1 Peter 4**

Hidden genius

Movie: *Music and Lyrics* (PG)

Clip details: The clip is the whole of chapter 5 on the DVD. It ends with the appearance of the video game character.

Synopsis: A washed-up old pop star finds hope in the hidden lyric-writing genius of the girl who waters his plants.

Summary

In *Music and Lyrics*, Alex Fletcher (Hugh Grant) is an ex-pop star who now makes a modest living doing 1980s reunions and performing at amusement parks. His fortunes change, however, when the world's biggest star ("bigger than Britney and Christina put together!") gets in touch. She's a big fan of his, and wants him to write a song for her new album.

This is great news for Alex, except for one thing: he's great at coming up with melodies, but he can't write lyrics. Enter his new "Plant Lady" Sophie (Drew Barrymore), who has an undiscovered natural ability in exactly the area that Alex is lacking. Immediately, he tries to recruit her to help him write the song, but

Sophie doesn't want to get involved. An evil ex-boyfriend broke her heart and shattered her self-confidence. As the deadline for the finished song approaches, Alex tries desperately to heal Sophie's self-esteem, and persuade her to help him write.

In this clip, Alex has hired a lyricist, but the relationship clearly isn't working – Alex is more used to writing ballads, whereas the lyricist writes words that are more suitable for heavy metal. Enter Sophie, who waters Alex's plants (including a plastic one) while coming up with her own lines for the song. Alex loves them – but now he will have a tough job persuading Sophie to use her lyrical gift.

OPENING UP

- Why do you think Sophie wants to turn Alex down? What do you think might be going on in her head?

- Later, Alex says Sophie has "been given a gift". What does he mean by this? Who gave it to her?

- What are some of your gifts and talents? What do you think you are best at?

- Do you have a hidden talent? Why don't you use it more?

- Tell at least one other person about a gift or talent you see in them – try not to go for the obvious.

TAKING IT TO THE WORD

Read 1 Peter 4:10–11

- What do these verses tell us about what our attitude to our gifts and talents should be?

- Do you think you use your gifts in this way? What does it mean to do so in practice?

- Why might it be important that Christians don't keep their talents hidden?

- Discuss how you and others around you can use the gifts and talents you have been given to serve God.

D23

THEME: **Innocence and responsibility**

BIBLE: **Galatians 6**

An innocent child?

Movie: *The Boy in the Striped Pyjamas* (12)

Clip details: The clip starts at 55 minutes and 30 seconds. It runs for 2 minutes, 20 seconds.

Synopsis: Almost without thinking, Bruno betrays his newfound friend, and so echoes the sins of his father.

Summary

One of the most memorable scenes from *The Boy in the Striped Pyjamas* sees two young boys, Bruno and Shmuel, sitting together separated by an electrified fence. Geographically, they are seated just a few feet from one another, yet, their situations are a million miles apart. Bruno's father is the Commandant of the fictional Nazi concentration camp in which Shmuel is a prisoner, yet, both of them seem unaware of what that really means.

In fact, neither of them understands anything of the gravity or consequences of Shmuel's situation. When his father goes missing, they assume he is innocently lost; when Bruno hears that his friend was brought in an inhumanely cramped train carriage, he can't understand why he didn't choose the half-empty and luxurious transport which he arrived in himself.

They are just children, caught up in the terrible schemes of men. Even as the Commandant's son, Bruno is innocent in the persecution of Shmuel and his people. Or, is he?

In this scene, Shmuel is brought to Bruno's home to clean glasses. Seeing his weak and malnourished friend, Bruno hands him some food, which Shmuel quickly stuffs into his mouth. Not quickly enough though; the mean soldier, Kotler has arrived to witness the Jewish boy with guilty crumbs around his mouth. When Shmuel claims that Bruno handed him food, the German boy denies ever having laid eyes on him. Like Peter denying Jesus, he has betrayed his friend when he needed him most.

OPENING UP

- What does this scene tell us about the "innocence" of youth?

- Is Bruno part of Shmuel's persecution as a Jew, or is he simply afraid to speak up?

- How do you think Shmuel felt? Why didn't he speak up?

- What do you believe you might have done in Bruno's situation?

- What might have happened if Bruno had spoken up in Shmuel's defence? Why do you think he lied?

TAKING IT TO THE WORD

Read Galatians 6:1–6

- What does this passage suggest about our responsibility to act when we see injustice?

- How can you practically speak up for people in your community who have no voice? What about in the wider world?

- Verse 4 is a helpful reminder that "all have sinned and fall short of the glory of God" – pray together that you will never become arrogant, or self-righteous, but always seek to become more like Christ.

D24

THEME: **Prayer**

BIBLE: **Ephesians 6**

A two-way street

Movie: *Evan Almighty* (PG)

Clip details: The clip begins 59 minutes and 50 seconds into the DVD. It runs for a 2 minutes and 30 seconds.

Synopsis: God explains to Joan that prayer isn't just like writing a letter to Santa – it's a two-way street.

Summary

A sort-of sequel to *Bruce Almighty*, this movie was panned by critics, yet received well by the church. It's hardly surprising – the movie is good, clean, faith-affirming family fun, and beneath a more obvious saccharine message about doing good to all, there are some more subtle theological reflections at its heart.

Evan Baxter (Steve Carrell), the tongues-speaking news anchor from *Bruce Almighty* has had a change of career, and is now a popular local politician. As the movie opens, we see him reaping the benefits of his new-found success, driving his perfect family to their huge new home – in a Hummer, of course. He's also a hit in the office, as he's been taken under the wing of influential Congressman Chuck Long (John Goodman).

Things begin to unravel, however, when God

(Morgan Freeman) chooses this inconvenient moment to ask Evan to build him an ark – Noah-style. At first, Evan resists, but God proves very persuasive, sending a series of mishaps to convince Evan of his calling. Eventually, he builds the giant wooden boat with the help of his family and a descending horde of animal pairs. When the weather takes a dramatic turn, the sceptical people of his town are suddenly glad he did.

In this scene Evan's wife Joan is talking to God – who has taken the form of a restaurant waiter. In the course of their conversation, God asks Joan how she thinks prayer is answered: "If someone prays for patience, do you think God gives them patience? Or, does he give them the opportunity to be patient?" They are the words Joan – who has begun to lose faith in her increasingly odd husband – needs to hear. She returns to Evan's side, and decides to believe in him; a wise decision, as it turns out.

OPENING UP

- What was the last thing you prayed for? What might be some common themes when you pray?

- Do you believe God answers prayer? Why or why not?

- What experiences have you had of God responding to prayer – either to you or those around you?

TAKING IT TO THE WORD

Read Ephesians 6:10–20

- What does it mean to "put on the armour of God"?

- Looking specifically at verses 19–20, what is Paul praying for?

- How might God answer that prayer, if *Evan Almighty*'s depiction of him is to be believed?

- Why did Paul need to ready himself with "armour" before praying that prayer?

- How would you like God to change your character? If you are prepared for him to surprise you, pray for each other, asking for these things.

D25

THEME: **Love**

BIBLE: **Luke 15**

A father's love

Movie: *Blood Diamond* (15)

Clip details: The clip begins 1 hour, 56 minutes and 30 seconds into the movie. It lasts for 2 minutes and 10 seconds.

Synopsis: An African boy-soldier, brainwashed by the rebels who kidnapped him, recognizes the unmistakable love of his father.

Blood Diamond is an important film, but it is not an easy one to watch. The themes, not to mention the language and violence, are very mature; yet, the film, like some of its characters, is dedicated to challenging the desperately important issue of conflict diamonds in Africa, and for that reason it should be applauded. With caution, we recommend this film for use with older youth groups who are serious about justice issues – but youth workers should always watch a film before showing it to young people.

Summary

African villager Solomon Vandy (Djimon Hounsou) has his world torn apart when rebel soldiers destroy his home, scatter his family and take him prisoner. He is put to work in the diamond fields, alongside other slaves, and risks his life when he discovers a huge gem worth millions of pounds. Solomon escapes, burying the diamond along the way, and sparking an international chase to find the stone. Once news of his discovery breaks, he is soon met by diamond smuggler Danny Archer (Leonardo DiCaprio), who wants to "help him" sell it.

Solomon's agenda is not profit-driven, however. He is only interested in finding his family, and when Archer helps him to do so, he realizes that his son Dia has been kidnapped by the rebels and brainwashed into becoming a child soldier. Solomon resolves that he will stop at nothing to rescue his son, and pursues him halfway across Africa, eventually snatching him from his military camp.

Dia has changed, however, and barely remembers his father. He has been turned into a killing machine, and even given a new name, "See no more". When Solomon takes his son, he has no idea what has happened to him. In this clip, the situation suddenly takes a turn for the worse, as Dia, believing the lies he was told about his family, picks up a gun and turns it on his father. Desperately, Solomon tries to persuade his son that he is "a good boy" who loves his parents. Broken and confused, Dia finally lowers the gun and embraces his dad.

OPENING UP

- How do you think Solomon felt to see his son aiming a gun at him? Might it have changed his love for his son? Why or why not?

- Why do you think Dia was pointing a gun at his dad? What might have been going on in his head?

- What do you know about conflict diamonds? How can we in the West put a stop to this awful trade? How can you impact the issue locally?

TAKING IT TO THE WORD

Read Luke 15:11–31

- This is a very different situation – but what are some of the similarities?

- How does the character of the father here echo the character of Solomon in *Blood Diamond*?

- What does it actually mean to you that God is your "Father"? How do you think he sees you and feels about you?

Index

YOUTHWORK MAGAZINE

Martin Saunders is the Editor of *Youthwork* magazine, the UK's most popular youth ministry resource. Every month, *Youthwork* is packed with resources, ideas and inspiration to help you in your work with young people. Each issue of *Youthwork* includes:

- an adaptable discussion starter, just like the ones in this book
- four session plans, rooted in the Bible and tackling key themes for young people
- movie clips from the latest DVDs, applied for your work with youth
- drama sketches, designed for use in a range of contexts
- in-depth updates on developments in youth culture
- longer articles by the world's leading youth work writers
- reviews of the latest resources
- stories from on the ground youth workers
- plus news, interviews, regular columns and more!

To subscribe now, and receive a great free gift, visit www.youthwork.co.uk/subscribe

Also by Martin Saunders:
The Ideas Factory

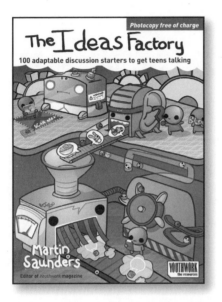

The Ideas Factory is a priceless resource for youth leaders.

The 100 spreads contain a story on the left-hand page, matched by questions on the right. Each explores a topic pertinent to young people, such as drugs, truancy, or parental relationships; or an important biblical concept, such as giving, the afterlife, or love. The questions begin with general issues, before moving on to what the Bible has to say.

The last 25 discussion starters provide a journey through the main stories and themes of the Bible.

"A rich resource for busy youth workers who want to connect issues of faith to everyday life." – **Jenny Baker,** writer

ISBN: 978-1-85424-834-3

Available from your local Christian bookshop.

In case of difficulty, please visit our website: **www.lionhudson.com**

Dave Wiles:
Stories From the Edge

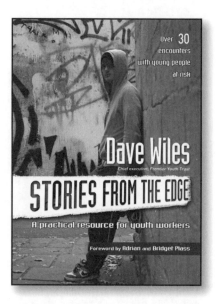

These true stories are instructive, inspiring, arresting and shocking.
• Meet the 16-year-old on probation, who is on suicide watch.
• Mediate between a rebellious youngster and his too-strict dad.
• Listen to a 21-year-old girl, with two children in care, who works the street to pay for the heroin her father deals.
Each chapter follows a particular theme, such as "Dads and Lads" or "Youth Culture and Gangs", and ends with points for discussion.

"Be warned – this book doesn't hold back; it is not a gentle read! Instead, it is full of tough stories and the reality of the lives of young people on the edge."
– Jill Rowe, Oasis

ISBN: 978-1-85424-936-0
Available from your local Christian bookshop.
In case of difficulty, please visit our website: **www.lionhudson.com**